A Force of Light

~ To illuminate your life's journey ~

Marina Petro

About The Author

Marina Petro has been working independently in the field of art and intuitive consulting and teaching since 1977. She is widely known for the clarity and depth of her intuitive 'readings.' Her clientele spans across the United States and over the seas to Europe, Japan and beyond.

Marina functions as a catalyst to help her clients restore harmony to their lives. The value of her service is the ability to 'see' into one's life and provide clear and useful guidance, information, and insight to the concerns and questions presented. She leads workshops and seminars in Intuitive Development, Intuitive Painting and other healing modalities.

Creating fine art, teaching healing and assisting others to discover and enhance their intuition, creative potential and spirituality is the hallmark of her work.

www.marinapetro.com
www.marinapetrofineart.com

INTRODUCTION

The content of this book was telepathically transmitted to me by an unseen intelligence. Most of it was received in sporadic early morning encounters from 1986 to 1991. The 'voice' that spoke into my mind seemed to be the spokesperson for a cluster of similar presences who would, at times, whisper "we are here" when they wanted me to receive and transcribe the next communication. They seemed to be more male essence than female.

The experience combined being compelled to write and not wanting to. The entirety of this work was done under great resistance. I had free will to refuse, but felt driven and prodded to continue. I could not be comfortable in my refusal so I wrote, or more exactly, transcribed. I still experience resistance coupled with deep abiding gratitude for the opportunity to experience the greater perceptual and spiritual understanding of our human experience that goes hand in glove with this type of encounter.

Throughout the body of this work the invisible source describes itself in a variety of ways. Early on when this process began, a transmission was given and I was told they are a group of five and I am one of them embodied. That I made a sacrificial journey to re-enter earthly existence and be the physical conduit for them. I get the feeling they, whoever they are, conspired and pushed me over the edge of a dimensional cliff when I wasn't looking. In the same transmission, they stated: "We choose to remain nameless. In remaining nameless you will have to familiarize yourself with our vibration so no deceiving entity can speak a name and call your attention to it." This would be likened to being blindfolded and led about a group of people, attempting to identify a specific person by sensing them. I accepted this and have not asked for a name.

Thinking back over my life, I can see indications that possibly led to my being a vehicle for these communications. As a very young child I remember hearing a voice calling my name and speaking within my mind. Accompanying it was the sense of a strong benevolent male presence. This would happen when I was alone and silent.

In conversations with other persons, or overhearing conversations, I would hear what the person speaking was saying, but another voice would also be present, in my mind, telling me what they were really thinking and feeling. I identified that voice as the voice of truth, or reality.

During my teenage years from about 14, I remember vivid conscious experiences where other worldly intelligences seemed to be communicating with me. There were spontaneous 'out of body' experiences which I didn't understand and told no one. Visions, which I told no one. I was not using drugs of any kind.

In July of 1977 I discovered I was psychic. As an adult, in the years surrounding my psychic opening, I experienced explosions of intense light in my head. There were other sporadic episodes with intense energies and light that would paralyze me as they roared through my body. At times I thought I would die when it was happening. I would often awaken from sleep with the experience of being with higher spiritual beings and taught throughout the night. With this came waking up to simultaneously reading and writing a book of spiritual teachings. I want to stress that I have not sought any of these experiences. I was not particularly spiritually oriented or motivated until my thirties after a long and terrifying episode of emotional and mental death and rebirth.

The discovery of my psychic talents happened in a very sudden experience which altered the course of my existence - or what I thought my existence was. At the time I was married and busy being mother to my three daughters who were 7, 10 and 12 and managing Awareness, Inc., a New York City and Connecticut based organization my husband, Robert, and I founded. Robert had become aware of his acuity as a psychic prior to my opening and was giving consultations and intuitive development trainings, out of which several gifted psychics emerged. I did not participate in the trainings. His classes were held evenings when I was home with our children.

One of my friends, a trained intuitive on our staff, invited me to accompany them to our New York office the next time they were offering an evening of mini readings. She knew I sensed colors around people and suggested I paint their colors and simply give them the painting. It sounded like fun and interesting. I agreed and went with them.

I could never have predicted what was about to transpire. I set up my easel, a pad of canvas paper and a few quick drying acrylic colors. My sole intention was to simply paint the colors I perceived and give the person the painting. This is no great artistic feat and relatively mindless. I've been described by some as a bit remote. I had no desire to speak, interact, or explain anything to them. I had no specific knowledge of what the colors meant, although I'd heard about the energy field, or aura, surrounding persons. I'd been sensing it all my life, but never paid attention or considered exploring it. I was too involved with the management of our organization, my family, and seizing the rare opportunities I had to develop my artistic talent which was then, and continues to be, one of the strongest drives in my life.

The first person who wanted her colors painted came into the room. She sat down in a chair facing me. I explained that I would be painting the colors I sensed around her and we fell into silence.

I focused my attention on her and immediately began to perceive colors, in my mind's eye, which I painted onto the canvas paper. After a minute or two, I noticed a voice within my mind, impressing me with information about her life. I ignored it. The impressions continued. I didn't want to get involved and continued to silently paint and ignore the gentle whisper. It persisted. I began to 'see' this woman in a variety of situations and realized I was experiencing her emotional states. It felt as if I knew this person without knowing her at all. I began to see and feel, in my own body, the areas of her body where physical disturbances were manifesting, relationships she was in, and the dynamics surrounding them. I was seeing into her past and her future as well.

I was being simultaneously taught what the colors meant and prodded to communicate the impressions I was receiving. I resisted until I could no longer resist and began to speak. It was as if a dam had burst and the stream of impressions were flowing through my mind and voice effortlessly. When I finished conveying the information, she confirmed everything I told her. I gave her the painting and she left.

Three or four other persons sat with me that evening and the process repeated with each one. I'd begin to paint, the flow of impressions would begin, and I would convey them. Each person confirmed the accuracy of what was given.

To ponder this, I suppose one would think I would be shocked or frightened with the sudden onset of this awareness. That was not my reaction. It felt completely natural, as if I'd been doing it all my life.

People began to seek me out for consultations and to teach. My primary work now is intuitive consulting, teaching and painting. The first two years I painted auras, believing it was the only way I could access this level of consciousness. When I discovered that by simply focusing my attention on a person and remaining receptive, the impressions would flow just as smoothly, if not more so, and I put my aura paintbox to rest.

Enough of my history. The transmissions in this book are in chronological order. One exception is February 4, 1991 which was placed at the beginning to illuminate the reader and set the tone. Part Two, "The Voice Of Silence" is a separate section of transmissions received during the healing meditation which closed an intuitive development, healing group I was leading at the time.

I've struggled with the idea of a table of contents. It was quite difficult to distill each transmission into a specific topic. Most seem to elude confinement and reach beyond the specificity the standard table of contents requires. The table of contents here is organized by each transmission number and, in most cases, part of the first sentence. When appropriate, I've listed a specific topic.

Read these transmissions slowly and contemplatively to extract their essence. The communications were received slowly and steadily - not at a normal conversational tempo. They were given at a pace that allowed me to write, pen to paper, enabling communion in silence in those early morning hours. Although I am an excellent typist, the sound and feel of either typewriter or computer felt objectionable.

I have experienced the love they speak of in these communions infusing me. May you also …

Marina Petro

TABLE OF CONTENTS

TRANSMISSION 1: FEBRUARY 4, 1991

In answer to the question: What is it that whoever is to read these words should know?

We wish you to know that we, as emissaries for the Divine Source, are with you. Do not perceive us as extraterrestrials for we are truly a part of the family of humanity's spirit, separated only by your undeveloped perceptual faculties.

We are the teachers you so earnestly seek in physical embodiment. Those teachers who you consider your masters on this plane are in unity with our vibration and essence. They hear and respond to our voice and are open to and able to transmit our energy essence of love. When they speak or emanate, it is we who are present - a universal force of unified intelligence expressing through their beings.

We wish you to know that we avail ourselves to you. We are ever present and accessible through your consciousness. You need only to know that we exist and open to our essence and silent communication.

We are the subtle inspirations which guide your lives

towards the highest good. We are the impressions you receive daily which challenge the negative beliefs and habitual responses which continue to keep you in bondage. We guide the way to freedom. We cannot interfere with your lives or decision making. We can only telepathically emanate our essence to inspire and guide.

Know that by reading, absorbing, and contemplating the words manifested within these pages, you will establish a connection with us and, ever so subtly, like a gentle wind, the wisdom and guidance contained within will be remembered and reawakened in your consciousness to teach and guide your lives as they unfold each moment.

We are with you. We are present. We surround you with our love. This is what we wish you to know.

TRANSMISSION 2: SEPTEMBER 25, 1986 (PERSONAL)

Telepathic Communication ~ Regarding my process

The meaning lies not in the manifested words, although they are partially our manifestation and your vocabulary and ability to express the impressions you are receiving. The meaning is transmitted, instantaneously and wholly, a moment before the flow of words in a beamed, non-verbal telepathic impression. Notice the pattern. Become aware of the rhythm and the variety in beams. Be aware of the initial impression, the seed impression which will precipitate the flow ~ like a piece of bait dangling just above a fish in the ocean. You see, my love, this is how we will train and refine your capacity to receive and accept. Do not reject our expressions of love to you and others. *(When I heard the words 'my love' I experienced resistance.)*

The words expressed in verbal or written form will never be adequate. Most channeling is an inadequate expression of the original thought. Even in the deeper trance states, rejection and altering takes place. Be aware and put resistance, fear, and pre-conceived concepts aside. We are bringing new information to be revealed in its simplest form through you. Await another energy/transmission encounter.

Over the years I have intermittently experienced sudden

and extremely intense surges of energy through my body which have immobilized/paralyzed me when they occur. It is a frightening experience and on more than one occasion I thought I was going to die while it was happening. I'm not sure if this is what the above sentence is referring to.

Your magnetic field will be penetrated by the 'Great One' that follows us. No harm will come to you. Let go to it. Resistance will make the process more uncomfortable. Rose, gold, white and silver will be stabilized in your energy field of manifested expression. Smoke will be dispersed. Notice afterwards the effect on others and the group entities who are then attracted to you by magnetic forces for balancing. You are a balancing rod, a tuning fork for those on the physical plane of manifestation, and not a word need be spoken. Your presence is the purifier, the tuning fork for others energies which silently affects the deepest stratum of their being.

In three years, your time, you will be emitting the most powerful rays of purification. The field will be brilliant white as the predominant energy pattern extending, with the lesser rays being automatically called forth to balance externals. Not a word need be spoken. Remember to go back to these notes for reinforcement.

Soon the words will be given fully for others and outward expression. Now we prepare you for understanding of your purpose as an extension of us. The 'Great One' we speak of is ever descending closer into and through the magnetic field of your Earth...*(interrupted by a phone call here.)*

TRANSMISSION 3: JANUARY 25, 1987

W e are the intermediate energy forms present, attuning you, familiarizing you with our flow of thought prior to the appearance and descent of the 'Great One' which is to follow us. There is no sense, at this time, in revealing its identity and characteristics, other than it is a cumulative force of God.

I perceived the following to be directed to my forthcoming Thursday night group:

We welcome you into our presence. You are gathered here, at this time, not knowing why. Not knowing what drew you here. Some of you believe that you are here to develop your psychic talents. Others believe that they're here to develop healing talents. Others, to hear spiritual truths, creative perspectives, in the hope to jolt your lives and your life experiences into other dimensions of perception...to take you out of your states of boredom, your states of chaos, your states of confusion. These are the superficial reasons why you come.

You have been drawn here because the soul within you, the God within you, desires freedom from the entrapment that has been placed upon it during your existence here on the physical plane. Now is the time to turn and face yourselves honestly, brutally honestly - examining your egos, examining the illusions you have created in your lives, examining the false concepts, the false truths that you have absorbed into your beings. Examining the patterning and the personalities that you have adapted and are using - living through others personalities that are not your own - that are based on others expectations of you from the time of your childhood and entry into this plane. Examining your needs for power.

Know that we are here simply to express he impulse of God - to express the universal flow - to express truths to the extent that they can be expressed and understood in physical form. Know that words will be inadequate. Know the direction and guidance you receive in words, receive as inspiration, that many of you leave here and feel an uplifting of your energies and come back week after week for more. Know that this is not enough. Know that each of you as individuals must take responsibility for your lives, for your existences here. Know that simply hearing words, becoming inspired, is akin to drug use. It's not enough. You must use what is being given in a deliberate, systematic way to alter your existences here in the physical.

Know that the next several. Years will be the most opportune time for all of humanity to align themselves with the God Force. Aligning yourselves simply through acts of meditation through any other practices is not enough. That is the beginning. That is the initial discipline. That is simply allowing space for the higher impulse of thought to find its way into your consciousness.

Taking action is necessary. When you realize what you perceive to be an inadequacy, an imbalance, a destructive behavior, you must take action to alter that behavior or habit and bring yourselves into alignment with the benevolent evolving forces of the universe. Pulling yourselves forward, going forth, leaving the states of inertia and self-destructiveness. This is how you begin to convince yourself that you love yourself. Most of you hate yourselves more than you love yourselves. You love yourselves for specific acts, for talents, for things that are glorious and wonderful that *others* can perceive in you. You seek to develop the traits that will please others - so others will say: 'You're wonderful' 'You're talented' 'You're beautiful' 'You're loving' 'You're compassionate.' This has no meaning on the inner spiritual plane. None! You're simply responding once again, even though it may be in a spiritual context, to the demands of society, to the programming of the mass consciousness of society which leaves you in the same state as when you began.

Begin in your homes. Begin with those close to you. Begin by truly learning how to love. Begin by accepting those that are close to you and respecting the essence within each one of them, which is God. Realize all the ways you seek to control them. Let your homes be your spiritual mystery schools. Begin by loosening the cords of control that bind you to those close to you. Allow them their own existences. Think not that you have the answers for them, regardless of what appearances may be. Live the principles of truth for yourself in your own life and do not try to force or teach others. They will be taught by your actions, by your responses.

When true love is emanating from your being, all will be in harmony for you. Realize the resentments that you hold to those close to you because they may not be capable of fulfilling needs that you may have. You want them to make you happy. You want them to agree with your thoughts. You want them for those purposes and when they can't respond, conflict is created within you. Hurt is created in you. Hostility is created within you simply because another being can't perform in the way that you wish them to perform; can't fulfill your needs. Know that no one on this planet but yourself can fulfill your needs.

Release from your consciousness the attitudes prefixed by the words or concept "if only." "If only they could be what I desire them to be." "If only they this, if only they that." It is a total waste of energy. Attend to what is. Accept what is. Attend to yourselves. Love yourselves. Align yourselves. Choose the benevolent for yourselves. Transform your own life. No one else can make you happy but you. Realize that all externals, and your own physical bodies, are temporary on this physical plane. Know that you carry with you, through eternity, yourself. That's all. Your essence. The soul within you. All else is transient.

Know that those who appear to be your adversaries - those who are your husbands, your wives, your lovers and your friends who seem to be catalysts for the turmoil and frustration in your lives - know they are your benefactors. Know that each one of them is helping you to move back and face yourself. They're telling you: "I can't make you happy. I'm doing the best I can." Do you realize? Do you ever truly realize that you don't know the ones that are closest to you" You don't know them. Do you know what's in their souls? Do you understand what has created them to be as they are? Do you understand them? And if you did you would accept them and wouldn't expect the impossible. Do you realize that your husband wife, child or friend might be, and probably is, from their perspective, thinking the same way as you. "If only..." wanting from you what you may not be able to give? And yet, we keep our pompous stand that we are the perfect ones; giving and giving and giving and getting so little in return. But do you really give? Think. Reach out to those that you want more from. Give more to them. Communicate with them. Let them open their hearts to your seek to know what is within them. This may be very threatening. If it is, the more reason to attempt.

Know we come to you in love. Know we come bearing principles, facets of reality that you may ponder, that you may choose to apply in your lives. When the sword of reality and truth comes down, many times those listening may be angry, may be threatened. The glass of illusion shatters and fear enters because the sword of truth and reality pushes those who hear it into a state of turmoil - into a state between worlds. Between what has been fixed as a way of life and the unknown - the void of unknowingness. But, know and rest that we love you. Know that when you choose the path of reality all else in your life converges into a higher order. We leave you now and thank you.

TRANSMISSION 4: MARCH 5, 1987

The Psychic Sense/The Mystical-Spiritual Sense

When we refer to psychic abilities we speak of a facility of the mind, the brain, which has nothing whatsoever to do with the spiritual or mystical sense or experience which is of a more encompassing nature. The psychic sense can be experienced by most persons through disciplined practice, through lowering or heightening the vibration of thought. It is a skill that can be trained and developed to varying degrees according to each individual's inherent capacities. The mystical or spiritual sense is an experience of the soul and cannot be trained. It can only be experienced.

Spiritual enthusiasm and euphoria, temporary highs, magnetic speakers and drugs can artificially stimulate the mystical/spiritual sense or the illusion of this sense. This is the road to fanaticism, akin to drug use. You can study read, hang on to the presence of a spiritual guru or teacher, eat rice and vegetables, meditate endlessly, pray endlessly, do your good deeds in the outside world serving others, never show anger, speak with a soft voice, live frugally, chant, light candles, observe holidays, become proficient in psychic abilities, yet never experience or maintain the spiritual sense, which is the knowledge and experience of the presence of God in your life and as your self.

The more you seek to be spiritual, the more elusive the experience becomes. You can perform all the outer acts and duties and not be an iota closer. You seek something that is already yours. You seek outside of yourselves for something that is your birthright. You seek to appear spiritual and perfect in the outside world and for others according to whatever the expectations of spiritual traits are currently popular. You move further and further away from yourselves, your true selves.

Think not for one moment that psychic abilities are an indication of spirituality. Spirituality is an ongoing process. You never 'get there' and stay there. Continual shifting, changing, higher and higher states of realizations are ever present.

Spirituality or enlightenment is self-knowledge, knowing yourself and allowing that self to express itself as it is. Acknowledging yourself as you are. Not pretending to be something artificial.

The greatest act you can do for anyone if you are seeking to 'help' them is to offer new perspectives, options that they may consider. Before you can do this effectively, you must search your own self and take the standpoint wherein you have no investment in the outcome other than the person's highest good and…you will never know what that is. Realize the greatest you can do is to stand by, allowing yourself to receive them when they choose to consult you. If you keep reaching out with your 'wisdom' to change them to your ways, nothing but failure for yourself and them can ensue. There can be no ties for this process to have optimum effect. Unconditional love, acceptance and willingness to allow another to live their life is the necessary prerequisite.

Know that each soul is a facet of God. Each has chosen to experience their own unique path of experience on the physical plane. You will never know why. Only the God within each individual knows why and is there, present through the entire experience of life; leading, prodding, present, waiting for the time to emerge in its fullness and be recognized.

TRANSMISSION 5: JUNE 11, 1987

*The following question was asked as a result of a group
discussion on spirit guides the night before.
Give me clarifying information on spirit guides. Do they
exist? What are they? How do they manifest?*

S pirit guides are a manifestation of the person's own
consciousness, drawn to the individual through an inner
call for help. In many cases, they are thought forms created
by the individual and empowered as an external energy, or
thought form, to have the answers that are already present in
the originators being - self-creations of, and for, what is
already known but desiring to be made conscious.

If one is fearful for their physical survival, the 'guide' who
is already present within (and empowered as if without) will
signal the physical entity through the subconscious mind. Spirit
guides will never interfere with any major event an entity has
to experience. Their presence will weaken/withdraw at the
command of the soul to lead the entity into and through any
experience necessary for its (the soul's) emergence as the
supreme power; seeking unity with God in man's conscious
awareness.

The soul within, in its own light, pushing outward and
upward as a seed planted in the earth in darkness is propelled

by its own forces of evolution to burst through the surface and into light. The soul seeks its perfect expression, which is the consciousness of God, planted within you since the beginning. It seeks full expression in each incarnation. It seeks to burst forth through the illusions, through the fears, through all that prevents its full expression in your life.

Seek then and encourage the emergence of God within. Give power to the God within you. No external guide can contain all the answers or protection you seek. And, by the very nature of its selective birth by your selective needs, can in some cases, limit your experiences, protect your body, rid your life of adversaries and guide you into a position of false power until enough experiences are avoided to call forth the guiding hand of the soul, your true guide, who's purpose is to experience fully. The soul, in its love for God and oneness with God will lead you into the storms, challenges and other situations to bring about the realizations necessary of anything that restricts the expression of you as the essence of God, or the free expression of God, in anything or anyone around you.

Examine your lives and what restricts you and what you restrict in yourself and others. Pay attention to all that you respond to with resentment and know that you poison yourself and the other each time you allow the feelings of resentment, criticism, restriction and fear. Know that you can live freely. Change and alter your own existences. Love yourselves enough to guide yourselves through the self-imposed prisons you've created.

If you've given others power in your life, begin to take back and claim your own power. Rule yourselves and you will teach those around you. Confront those you've given power to and stand in your own light. Give them the opportunity to realize as well. If you continue your self-destructive, self-imprisoning relationships and patterns you will continue to sink into the mire of your negative emotions which will continue to energize and magnify each situation until a crisis is called forth to awaken you.

Look back upon the crises in your lives and realize the components that brought them into being. When energy is contained beyond the capacity of the container that holds it, it must burst forth beyond the limits of what is containing it…hence the crisis.

TRANSMISSION 6: JUNE 16, 1987

The greatest adversary you can ever encounter in your life's journey on the physical plane is fear. Fear is the Great Destroyer of your hopes, your dreams, your aspirations. Fear is the Great Destroyer of the harmony within your relationships. Fear of loss, fear of failure, fear of life, fear of the next moment. Most of you live your lives (your lives being the thought that you manifest) projecting fear into each and every situation you encounter. Projecting the negatives of what could go wrong and allowing those negatives to overpower the positive and forward moving momentum of whatever the situation is that you're contemplating.

Your fears travel like dark arrows through your mind and being, interpenetrating every encounter, every situation, every thought; poisoning and limiting your existences on this physical plane.

You are here to manifest the expression of God. You are here to manifest all that you can become fearlessly. The inner promptings that rise up within your mind giving you those bursts of enthusiasm, those bursts of light, those bursts of the next step, those bursts of insight into your potential, your creativity. The goals, the direction that you're seeking is always there - right on the perimeter of your consciousness. You all have dreams of what it is you wish to manifest. Where do you think those dreams originate? They originate from the guide that you so eagerly seek outside yourself that lies within you, always present, always expressing itself through you and attempting to manifest its beauty, its creativity and its purpose on this physical plane. Your guide, being the essence and the oneness of God, The Creator.

The Creator, the creative sense within you, is endlessly expressing the highest you can become at any given moment. It is always manifesting ideas and filtering them through your consciousness. Where do you think those thoughts originate? Listen closely to those sparks of enthusiasm, to those sparks of direction and pay heed to them. Each one that rises in your consciousness is the revelation of another facet through which you can express your creativity in this lifetime and realize the fulfillment that you seek. How many times have these gems risen within your being to guide you? How many times have you felt that spark of enthusiasm, that wonderful energy, that wonderful momentum of creativity and thankfulness? You are sparked and then sit and ponder all the ways it cannot be made to manifest. You sit and project failure through your minds. You do not place yourselves in the situation as successful. The original thought gave you the feeling and the sense and the entirety of the situation along with the feelings of success.

When we speak of success, we do not necessarily mean success in the outer world or success and acclaim from others. We mean success and fulfillment within yourself. Where you have put into manifestation and created something that would give you pleasure, that would give you joy, that would bring you out of the limitations and the boredom that you dwell in much of the time. You allow limiting, negative fear to enter right at the inception of your potential creations. Or, if you do begin and tell others about it, you accept any negativity, limiting thoughts, warnings or dangers from them to enter your consciousness and create limitation within once again.

You place the harnesses of fear before you. These harnesses now must be loosened and put behind you. What do you have to lose? Think carefully on that question. Whatever it is, place it against the gains that can be achieved through accomplishing and manifesting your goal. Look back upon your lives. Look back at the wonderful, wonderful ideas that were given to you by yourself, by the God within you, which is your thought. Think carefully and remember the thought process that brought you to the decision not to go forward and create the manifestation, the idea.

It is not important to achieve for the eyes of the outside world. It is important to achieve and express your creativity and all that you can become for yourself and only for yourself; and if that creation touches and affects other people's lives, that's fine and wonderful, but it's you that needs to be fulfilled. It's you that needs to express your creativity outwardly within the context of your life span.

Most of you don't even realize the fears and the limitations. You've gotten so used to thinking and responding in that way. When someone outside yourself tells you of their plans or a new venture, how does your mind accept it? Think about what your initial reaction is. Is it uplifting and encouraging for the person, or do the thoughts of fear, limitation and failure enter with their lightening fast arrows? And as they enter, that thought, that impression, is instantly transmitted to the other person and doubt enters them as well, putting a bit of poison into their enthusiasm if they accept it. If they accept enough, and if they speak enough to enough negative minded persons, the plan will more than likely fail or be much more difficult to achieve. Realize how you poison others and take responsibility for your own. Also, know who you speak to when you express.

Think back and make a list of all the wonderful ideas that came to you that you pondered for brief periods of time and never put into manifestation. The ones your mind continues to go back to in sorrow and remorse. Make a list and then make a list of the thought processes and reasons why you didn't move forward with the inner directed goal. Make your lists until a pattern of understanding emerges for you. What will emerge is the atmosphere of failure, the atmosphere of fear, the atmosphere of 'what if's' the atmosphere of limitation, the atmosphere of inertia - the force that binds.

So, you're given wonderful ideas, wonderful creations from your wonderful inner being to manifest on the physical plane to fulfill yourself, to fulfill what you came here to fulfill - to create, to bring forth. And you sit and ponder all the ways you can fail. You attempt to see the entirety of the situation from the one manifesting thought which has already given you the entirety of the situation. You allow yourselves to become overwhelmed. You begin to see the creation as drudgery, as fear, as 'how am I going to do this or that or the other?'

Look at your creations as great adventures. Know that if you point your ship, focus and put all your attention and energy into it, that the universe is there to provide you with the next step and with all the energy you need to continue to bring your thought into manifestation.

TRANSMISSION 7: JUNE 17, 1987

W hen one begins to enter the higher states of consciousness, the heightened states of realization and consciously experiences the first inflow and presence of universal thought and intuitive insights that come when the mind and being are aligned with the higher vibrating energies of the universe (*the energies emanating from the planets, the inrush of energy of the sun and the particles of intelligence that inter permeate all*) cellular changes begin to take place in the person's system. The electromagnetic field, within and surrounding the person, gradually begins to vibrate on a finer level which begins the process of change and the evolution of consciousness that nothing else could evoke in such a way.

The onset of this process is usually precipitated by a crisis in one's life. A situation that calls the person beyond the limits of their ordinary understanding and forces the mind to seek beyond itself for solutions, respite from the confusion, the pain, whatever the situation is, whatever the puzzle is. The mind begins to send, both outside of itself and from deeper resources and recesses within itself, the call for assistance, the call for understanding; the silent and sometimes desperate prayer to bring balance and harmony back into the being.

When the call for balance and harmony is sent out and recorded within, both the forces within the being and the forces without, respond simultaneously, creating a merge and an alignment. When God is call upon, it responds. When a question is asked, the answer is present and is brought into the awareness of the entity according to the level of receptivity open at the time.

When the first connection is consciously made, a different sense is felt and recorded within the being; a sense of harmony, a sense of something greater than the prior experiences felt, the sense of a subtle presence, the sense of guidance and a sense of awe.

For the most part, unbeknown to the entity, according to their level of awareness and consciousness of the existence of higher realms that can be accessed, the desire is born to experience more; simply because it is one of the highest experiences that can be realized within the being. One of the purposes for existence on this physical plane is to make contact with the higher self, to align the person with the energy, harmony, and the thought impulse of God. The desire is born to experience more of that sensation where universal mind has seeped through into conscious awareness, no matter how subtly, and begins to permeate the presence, begins to vibrate more strongly in the person's aura and interpenetrates the being. It avails itself to the individual and magnetically attracts more of its essence to the individual. It's there, present at all times but it takes the initial call, the initial desire of the individual to go beyond. The more intense the call, the more inrush of energy - the breaking through of the seed into the outer form.

In everyone's life a situation unfolds that enables this birth to take place. Such is one of the guaranteed experiences of the physical plane - the Great Mystical Crisis - the opportunity to become one with the consciousness of the

Creator. The opportunity to fulfill the purpose of life on Earth. Each time the soul enters the physical plane, it is with the inner knowingness that this and these events will take place in the lifetime. It's these grand events of upheaval that call forth the conscious alignment of the being with the mind and intent of its Creator. Look then upon your own times of upheaval, of confusion, and those that are taking place in other's lives as the sacred opportunity to align in thought and intent with the all loving, all creative, all knowing essence and consciousness of God. Know this to be true for yourself. Know this to be true for those outside of yourself.

We are currently entering a time of an accelerated call from the mass of humanity, consciously and unconsciously. The energies within all life systems, not only human life, have begun an acceleration process. There is more fear existing on this planet at this time than ever before. There's more confusion, more unrest; thus the greater the call for harmony, the greater the call en masse for clarity, the greater the call en masse for comfort and guidance. The call intensifies moment by moment as we exist in these present times. The response comes stronger and stronger, greater and greater to awaken humanity to align with its source.

Every individual currently conscious will experience an inrush of this greater permeating intelligence. Those who are already awakened to the knowledge of the process of the evolution of consciousness and the spiritual realities will have an easier time integrating the heightened vibrations within their being. But even these entities will be thrown into states of confusion, bombarded by the very thing that they're consciously calling to.

Those who have not awakened, who are still seeped in

the belief that they are unto themselves on this planet will have the most difficult experiences, which will eventually, whether this lifetime or in their intermediate states of non-physical existence when this lifetime has passed, be drawn back again with a heightened awareness with the seed of the conscious knowledge that there is a consciousness beyond the limited consciousness they acknowledge now on Earth.

Every being existing on this Earth now is being awakened in a way that has not taken place before. Every being who will leave their body (in death) will now *(either with conscious awareness, or make the transition and shortly thereafter in the non-physical- realms)* realize these principles and begin the fulfillment of their purpose in the following lifetime. This has never happened before.

TRANSMISSION 8: JUNE 18, 1987

I asked: What do you wish to express through me?

We wish to express the glorious attributes of God. We wish to express how persons can become all that they can be.

The creative impulse is one of the highest experiences a being can have in their lifetime. When the creative impulse is felt and experienced, it is one of the closest ways of being attuned and in tune to the intent and the attributes of your Creator, God.

You are here as an expression of God. You are here as a facet of God and you are here to manifest and create all that you can become and all that you are. The creative impulse is an integral part of each living life form. All life forms are in the process of creating and becoming all they can be. When one sits in contemplation of themselves, they are creating. When one speaks, they are creating. When one thinks, they are creating. All your actions are creative actions. All your thoughts are creative thoughts, and your external life is the fruition of your creativity, born through the womb of your consciousness; reflecting the exact replica of your internal world of intent, thought, emotion and attitudes.

We are here to extend to you, and awaken once again within you, the golden thread that leads back to your Creator. You are all Gods creating your universes. Your planet is essentially a school for Gods. Each one of you born with the seed of perfect love, all knowledge, all power, deep within your beings. You are here, and through your continual trial and error in your manifestations, are seeking to manifest the perfection of harmony, of love, on the physical plane. The God within you, *that you are*, continually seeking to express itself in your outer world.

At this point I began to speak into the recorder:

We are here as the higher existing energy patterns of your race of humanity. We are a light form that is part of the Godhead, part of the great power of universal harmony and creativity. We are as tuning forks who have been compelled through magnetic forces of disharmony to be called forth and emanate among you.

Our intent is simply to be what we are among you; which is the essence of what you are to become. We put forth a vibration and in our putting forth, those that are touched will awaken and their energies will harmonize with ours.

We are a universal force composed of non-physical beings, who at one time, had physical identities in a variety of life forms on your earth and beyond your earth. We have transcended the cycles of physical existence/manifestation. We have perfected our thought and intent. We have been reabsorbed into the light of the One and have been thrust forth again and reborn as units of intelligence emanating the attributes of God. We cluster in groups and at intervals, parts of our group agree to make the sacrificial journey back to the physical plane to re-experience, to enable us to express our intent through the spoken words the written world.

We have no relationship whatsoever with the lower vibratory forms of non-physical personality energy patterns who manifest as units of personality essence influencing human consciousness - some of which were highly accomplished in the arts, sciences, and politics in their sojourns on earth and desiring to influence, through telepathic transmission, the continuation of their earthly existence to those who are receptive, without entering into physical form, as they await the conditions most propitious for re-entry into the physical.

Transmission 9: August 1987

What is love?

Love in the purest sense is rarely experienced in physical existence from one being to another. Love is complete harmony. Love radiates outward. It cannot be contained or withheld. The nature of love is expansive. The greatest beauty. It asks nothing. It simply is. It exists. It is complete within itself and needs nothing to perpetuate its existence.

When you fall 'out of love' you were never 'in love' in the first place. Love is eternal. It cannot stop. It cannot be destroyed. Love is God. God is love; the fabric of the universe.

You are here to align yourselves with, and become love. Love enables complete freedom and acceptance of others and yourselves. It does not control. It does not manipulate. It has no ulterior motive, nothing to 'prove' to itself or another. Love is the greatest healer, the only healer. It simply is what it is, and whatever and whoever is within its presence heals, benefits in some way known or unknown. It speaks to its essence and listens with its essence. It does not judge or try to change another. It knows its power *must* bring change, but not how the change will come about - only that it is good.

TRANSMISSION 10: AUGUST 1987

———— ⚜ ————

Inner Peace is a state of knowingness that all is well. The internal/external balance between polarities of evolution and inertia. When one has mastered the subconscious being within and allows it to respond with acknowledgment of its existence, regardless of the eternal situation, there will be the experience of peace.

The road is through establishing communication with the God Self within. Knowing that each situation you find yourself in is transitory, both the pleasant and unpleasant, and yet, neither is to be avoided. Knowing that every storm passes, no matter its intensity.

Extend your vision. Life is becoming greater with each passing moment. If you could but see the changes in each passing moment throughout the universe - if you could but experience one full moment with full vision of how all is becoming all that it can be, it would be the ultimate experience of joy, faith, love and trust in the loving presence of creation and the wonder and adventure of life.

TRANSMISSION 11: AUGUST, 1987

S eek the eternal. Let your vision extend beyond the temporal. Whenever you are caught within the grip of any one situation, a cage exists for you. Yesterdays cages have disintegrated and you've walked into a new cage today. Do not allow the journey of your lives to go from existing from one cage to the next. Extend your vision. Your cage today is changing this moment. Each moment brings new thought, new awareness - the ever moving force of the creative universe rearranging, expanding. Move and flow with it.

Know there is the all-good existing in each situation that seems to trap you. Know this and extend your vision. Think not that you can determine another being's action or what is best for them. You cannot know. You cannot judge which experiences someone else must have to come to the realizations within that they are creators. You can remind them that they are creators when you know this within yourself. Know when you are embroiled in any upsetting situation, the spirit of creativity and transformation is also present.

Moment by moment apply these principles in your life and in relationship to others:

Love yourself.
Respect the intelligence within yourself and others.

Judge not.

Realize all are doing the best they know how at any given time.

Know all is moving in rhythm with the evolutionary forces of creativity

Resist not.

TRANSMISSION 12: SEPTEMBER 19, 1987

I sat by the tape recorder in an attempt to avail myself for a transmission and became so tired I had to lie down. When I did, the question below was given to me. I slept on and off the entire afternoon, which is very unusual. I asked the question when I woke up.

What does man need to experience in order to become one?

Mankind as a cumulative force and entity is in a very sorry state. Fear is rampant over your world. The greatest vibration being manifested at this time is fear. Your fears originate from the illusions created in your minds. Your fears, for the most part, are unfounded. Your fears are projections of the worst that could happen to you. You're so engrossed in the worst that can happen to you that you barely put any time or energy into thinking of the best that can happen to you. The negative is overpowering the positive. Is there no wonder that most of you are encased in shells of fear?

Know that your mind and your thoughts create your entire existence. Know that your fears are unfounded. How many of the actual projections have come to pass in the ways you have projected them? As long as the positive remains in the background and the negative takes priority, none of you will achieve your desired goals. None of you will achieve your dreams.

The time is now to search your minds and yourselves and face the reality that your fears are unfounded. You have died countless times in your minds. Your loved ones have left you countless times in your minds. Your loved ones have died. Your loved ones have been in accidents. Your loved ones and everything in your radius has been projected into a state of fear. You will die once. Those you love will die once, and yet you experience either their death or whatever it is that you project on to them many times in your lifetime. You live it in your mind. You panic yourselves. There's no basis for the actuality. You live in the past. You project your fears into the future. Where are you now?

Fear and mistrust have been ingrained in your consciousness. You have accepted the belief that others can hurt you. You have given your power away as individuals to whoever and whatever you've allowed yourself to become attached to or want to keep in your life. You cling. You identify always with externals and give your power outwardly to the external, losing parts of yourself and your own identity in the process.

You label yourselves as 'wife,' husband,' whatever your profession is. All of you have labeled yourselves and in the process of labeling yourselves you limit your experiences and you limit the expansiveness and adventure that this lifetime can hold for you.

You have separated yourselves from your source of life and creativity and fallen into fear. You have lowered yourselves and accepted the fallen state of limitation, disease and a base survival consciousness.

You've all been given gifts. Each of you was born into this Earth Plane with a gift. Even those gifts have been cast by the wayside because of fear, limitation, self deprecation. You seek out others to enjoy and marvel at their gifts and ignore your own. Seek to discover your gift and manifest it. If all would turn to their creative consciousness, your individual lives and the world would be at peace.

While in the body you will never fully understand the mechanism of yourself and the full nature of consciousness. As humans you are like a fetus within the womb. You are to us as you are to the life beneath the oceans of which you can influence and observe, but for the most pat remain unobservable by them. When you jump into a body of water you are the extraterrestrials to the life therein as we are to you. But we are all one, in one world, born from one Creator and separated by the perceptual veils that exist.

TRANSMISSION 13: OCTOBER 6, 1987

Received while having my morning coffee.

We are here. We welcome you and thank you, once, again for your acknowledgement of our presence. We are to become a major part of your thought pattern, Marina, making transmission one with greater ease, but also greater questioning on your part as to when we are present and remnants of your ego-self are present.

We wish to speak about the power of subconscious projection. All life is in an illusory state. The strongest thought pattern being brought into conscious awareness through the lower unconscious aspects of impulse - the survivor within. Think about your lives and the quality of thought for a moment. Is not the majority, if not the whole of it, and your actions, based on survival of your form in one way or another? The maintenance of finances and projection of loss of them, the food you eat, the loves you have, the fears you imagine of losses which occur even for things you have not yet acquired or manifested? You stop your loftiest manifested creations while they are still being born in your mind. Your God gives you creative thoughts. They emerge constantly from the higher realms of your being and are then attacked by your fears. The battle is constantly being waged within you. And then you sit defeated, frustrated, at the mercy of a computer you yourself have programmed to stop you.

Your soul chose your present existence when in a non-physical state for the creative opportunities that were most propitious and not for the challenges of karmic retribution. For what you wanted to create, not to suffer for. Do you choose your jobs or work now for the hardships or for the benefits? We are here to tell you that your frustrations will increase unless you begin to take action on your creative impulses.

Each of you has an internal scanning device which lives in the lower unconscious and constantly scans your environment for evidence to maintain its beliefs for security. The lower unconscious does not like change. It cares naught for change. It is happy as it is. The unknown is fought constantly. Your freedom exists in what has not come into being and the unknown, change. If you are happy and joyous now, you have already found the key to the freedom of existence and you are fearless. But if not, do you not realize that freedom will come in the evolving changes that occur?

Know that the universe/God supports and loves you and will impersonally bring into your life the strongest of your existing desires or fears. Your desires are energy; real and tangible. They magnetize their replica to you through your life experiences. Your beliefs are energy and will also create what is real for you in your outer world. Your fears are also energy, and if your fear or subconscious protective impulse is stronger than what you think you desire, your fear will intervene and prevent the experience.

Your thoughts, beliefs, fears, joys and creativity are the substance which attract and solidify matter to you in the form of their likeness through experiences and persons. At any given moment in your life, you are able to see the state and stage of your self, made manifest, in your outer world. A perfect mirror. You may have to go through lifetimes experiencing a fractional part of your creative desires and beset with manifesting and living through the patterns of held fear and limitation until you see into the mirror clearly. Until the dawning comes when you experience (either in physical or non-physical form) the uselessness of it all and make the Grand Alignment in your consciousness and step off the rocky obstacle course of fear and inertia into the ever forward moving stream of life, creativity, light and faith.

Faith is love and knowing of the existence of God. Faith is knowing the nature of God. And if God could speak to you now, he would say:

"I am here, ever present, waiting to respond to your every call as I do. I watch over you as a parent watches their children stumble and fall as they learn. As I watch, my presence and strength engulf you but I cannot intervene until I am recognized and asked. You run in circles with your heads down. You run into the walls of your own creations and I watch and wait for the moment when you run fast and furiously enough to fall on your back and face me, recognize me, and ask for my guidance. Only then can I make my presence *consciously* known to you because only then have you recognized me. And so I wait, present, ever present. My thought and impulse of your perfect manifestation always part of you as you are part of me. You are me. I am you. I am your breath. I am your life. Turn to me. To the extent you recognize my existence, I will fill you with my essence and love.

TRANSMISSION 14: OCTOBER 7, 1987

———— ·❦· ————

Received during my Thursday night group after an
initial group meditation:

Each of you here and all those who are consciously aware
and consciously pursuing the spiritual realities, moving
along in the conscious evolution of themselves, have had
what is called a 'sacred wound' take place at some point in
their lifetime. Regardless of what it was, it is that place
within you that doesn't seem to heal. The one that keeps
coming back bleeding, that keeps coming back to remind
you of its presence. Through that wounding was the catalyst
to put you onto this path. Look at it as sacred, not something
to be shunned or as weakness. Don't use it to feel sorry for
yourselves, to pity yourselves, to cry for yourselves to pull
yourselves down. Don't use it to put fear in front of you.

So many of you, because of your past experiences, take
that fear, that event that happened in the past and put it in
front of you and that colors your entire existence.

The whole of what is trying to be brought forth in the
new time of awareness that's coming is that you all live in
fear. You all live in states of illusion and your illusions take
place because of events that happened in the past, hurts that

happened in the past and projecting those into your future, negating the now. You're not living now and it's important this be recognized within each one of you.

You can put up your defenses and say, "not me" but begin to examine your lives. It is very important. It is important to examine your lives and clear the veils of fear from your vision. Each one of you here are healers in one capacity or another. Each one of you has tremendous creativity you haven't even begun to scratch the surface of. It is that creativity, and I don't mean focusing on artwork or photography, although they are included, I mean using the creative mind to bring forth and manifest your potential in this world. That's what you're here to do.

Ask yourselves right now as I'm speaking, and I'll give you a moment to think about it when I say this: If you had six months to live, what would you do? What would you get rid of? What would you stop doing? What would you do? Think about the time wasted in fear alone; in contemplating fear. In stopping experiences that your soul is calling you forth to experience because of fear, self-deprecation, lack of confidence, fear of people, fear of judgments onto yourself - whatever the case is - fear of failure. It is these fears that need to be seen crystal clear and be recognized as illusions.

And, if there is a Satan in this world, it is fear. Solely fear, in the myriad ways it manifests in your lives. If there is a Satan or an evil in this world, it is the rehashing of all the past, the remorses, the guilts from the past and the projected fears into the future which keep the lid on your lives now.

Whatever it is that has come into your mind lately as a creative idea, and you've all had them - something fruitful, something that you can express your humanitarian instincts, your creative instincts, anything that is going to bring you out and bring joy and openness into your lives. Take the steps to bring that into manifestation. Open the barriers that have become habitual prisons, and the prison is worse because it is not seen, it is felt, it is not seen.

This is why awareness needs to take place in this area. Know that when you take the steps that will move you beyond the boundaries you've imposed on yourselves, whatever they may be (and you all know what they are because you all have them) When you take those steps beyond the invisible boundaries then the higher self and the higher mind, the God Self is there with you opening things even more.

But you, the human being, as the physical entity, need to take action, physical action, and reach out beyond yourselves if you want to break patterns and if you want to open your lives. Taking those risks can only bring benefits to you.

If you could see yourselves as wonderful, wonderful beings to be shared with others. You have something of value, the beauty within you, that is what you need to see; the beauty within yourselves. Allow it to be shared with others, shared with strangers. You want new people, new friendships in your lives and yet how many of you are afraid of strangers? How are you going to establish new friendships if you're afraid of strangers? It's those risks you need to take.

TRANSMISSION 15: OCTOBER 17, 1987 (PERSONAL)

We welcome you into our presence. You are like a wild stallion running from every restraint or imagined restraint as we approach you in consciousness. You are believable. This is why you are perfect for receiving our conveyances. You have forgotten you are one of us. If you could see yourself, you would see the reality of yourself running from yourself, running from your best friends. We shall all have a good laugh with this stage once you have re-entered our dimension and re-joined with us. We promise this will become easier, almost enjoyable for you - rebel that you are - always have been.

We are entering and influencing some of those around you. New persons being brought into your radius shortly to assist. Be open and aware, non judgmental. You must avail yourself to us or the frustration you experience will magnify. We must manifest. It is for your ultimate benefit. The freedom you seek in this earthly life will become a closer perceived reality. You have willingly agreed. Now stop the fight. Put your fears aside and step aside. The very thing you seek will be given through this experience of moment to moment communion with us.

I think: I don't know where I (Marina) begin and end anymore?

They answer: You begin in the farthest reaches of space and light. You are endless. Allow the multidimensional nature of who you are. Do not fight it. Most mental illness stems from the fight, resistance, and fear of one's multidimensional nature. Allow, allow, allow. Observe. Write. Only through experimenting and practice will you trust. You keep putting dams up to stop the very thing which will free you. You need no other teacher but what will be transmitted through you. Each step of the way we are there. We have the same difficulty experiencing your resistance to the highest as you do when your human mind is open to other beings in your readings. So clearly you see how blindly they run from the most benevolent. Stop questioning. No one else has to see what you do.

TRANSMISSION 16: OCTOBER 25, 1987

———————— ❦ ————————

There is a level of consciousness that is not yet known, not yet discovered by human entities. The new children being born into the Earth Plane, at this time, will begin to exhibit the tendencies of lightness, defying of gravity and the ability to transfer physical material into ethereal and ethereal into physical.

We are here to tell you that the world Earth, as you know it, is about to take a dramatic change within the next 15 years, your time. What you perceive as reâlity and the basic physical laws of matter, gravity, and anti-matter are about to take a radical shift, leaving your scientific minds in disarray. What they (scientists) haven't taken into consideration are the shifts taking place in the electromagnetic spheres surrounding Earth as a culmination of the natural and forced bio-gravitational events currently taking place.

Higher frequency sound waves and sound waves in general will become more intense, travel and penetrate other magnetic fields, including human. Computers and the heightened use of computers and the intrusions into energy fields, as a mass consciousness within themselves, becoming a stronger force of thought. The cris-crossing lines of mass electronic communication systems are affecting life by interfering with natural energy fields and the protective barriers surrounding them. Signals, intrusions, constant bombardment from external sources are allowing more incoming data to penetrate the protective energy fields surrounding (especially) human life than the human system can integrate and keep balanced. Disorders of the nervous system caused by high frequency energies/sound waves, interfering with brain patterns causing the brain rhythms to be set into erratic patterns affecting the systems of the body.

The Earth itself is reacting in correspondence in revolt. If the Earth could speak, it would say: "You have raped me. You have destroyed the beauty of my being. You are weakening me daily; taking and building beyond may capacity to give and to maintain myself. I am grieving deep within my being. I cannot withstand my grief or your intrusions and I must reject you for my ultimate survival. I am weakening at a pace that has reached unprecedented proportion. I will no longer sustain your intrusions. My body hurts. I am an entity with a soul. I am alive. I need to rest. I can no longer rejuvenate. I am in confusion. I was once whole and in perfect harmony and must return to my original state. I have no voice to speak. I am trying to tell you through the eruptions in my body. I am about to rebel and cast you away for my survival. I am innocent."

Transmission 17: November 10, 1987

This was received spontaneously after a brief attunement. I'm still feeling quite a bit of resistance and difficulty disciplining myself to sit.

We welcome you into our presence. We wish to offer further information regarding what the *Coming Of The Lord* means. The way is being made clear through human consciousness presently permeating the globe of your Earth. The amount of fear, panic, the conscious and subconscious calls outwardly for help, are drawing to the Earth plane a very high key magnetic energy influence. Never before in the history of your Earth has such a profound calling out manifested. Knowingly or unknowingly, wittingly or unwittingly, the masses of humanity and nature are in distress and calling out for balance, harmony, peace, love, relief.

Yours was a world that was meant to live in harmony. You, as supposedly higher forms of nature, were placed with the animal life, all natural life, so that you might learn from the rhythmic harmony of existence. So that you might see that all of nature works interdependently, effortlessly, joyously, when left to its own natural rhythm and devices. Mankind has altered the balance of nature and has disregarded and not learned from the effortlessness of nature. And now, all of your Earth is in great stress and disharmony and our call is being heard. The convergence and descendence of the mind of the Creator is drawing closer and closer into the atmosphere and will permeate all life on Earth and influence all life physically and through consciousness.

We are here as intermediary energy forms attempting to awaken humanity to a higher form of life and existence. We are here emitting our energy fields in preparation for the great outburst of light and consciousness which is descending ever closer into your Earthly atmosphere. Never before has such a great thrust in awakening the masses taken place. We are not able to prevent destruction. We cannot stop the hand or the mind who would decide accidentally or deliberately to destroy much of your Earth through nuclear devastation. We cannot stop the natural processes of the Earth itself as the entity and soul, and being that it is, from expressing its rebellion. We can only emit what we are, which is a reflection of the 'Great One' who rules supreme. We are the messengers.

The king is returning to his kingdom. The mother returning to her child. God is turning to face humanity. And what will they find? And what will they look for? They will look for affinity. They will look within the hearts of those existing on the planet and will take into their hearts, absorb into the One, only that with which there is an affinity. Only those in which the spark of love has been born. Those who know there is no death. Those who have been waiting with heart and eyes and arms outstretched. Those children of God, who know they are children of God, and who are known as children of God by what is in their heart, will be infused and will know in an even deeper way, that their Father, Mother, Lord has come to take them home.

Home is the alignment with the energy field that will be emanating at that time. Home is not a place of physical existence. Home is the alignment of the being with its Creator through the energy and consciousness that will be permeating the Earth at that time. And when physical death comes, they will be quickly reabsorbed and lifted on a beam of light into the pool of love and creativity. They will not be trapped in the lower emotional planes of non-physical existence. This is how the prophesied separation will take place.

Those who do not acknowledge and whose beings are steeped in guilt in fear, in greed, in hatred, in selfishness, in retributive anger, will experience intensification of these characteristics in very severe ways. Whatever is being held within, both the light and the dark, will be intensified as the process of purgation takes place. Intensifying of the harmful, destructive tendencies will bring either their own destruction or will force higher awareness and alignment. In either case, it will be through the magnification and rapid karmic reaction of thought and action that will be brought quickly into the lives of those, so they may have the opportunity to experience physically, and in an immediate way, the destructiveness and the imbalances that lie within - the results of their harbored feelings, attitudes, thoughts and actions. The Great Teacher is here.

Seek then to know yourselves. Turn within. Join with others where you can elevate together. Form your groups. Turn within. Purify yourselves. Know yourselves. Acknowledge the forces of destruction within. Acknowledge them with a brutal awareness and transform them with conscious deliberate effort.

Bring into your lives that which will nourish you. Break the veils of fear, illusion, inertia. Feed your minds and hearts with light, with love, with optimism, with faith. Program yourselves. Reprogram yourselves. And as the new enters, the destructive will emerge and disperse. But be aware and consciously take control. Reach out beyond yourselves. Do not isolate yourselves. Be among others. We leave you and thank you for your attentiveness.

TRANSMISSION 18: NOVEMBER 13, 1987

This was received verbally. I spoke into the tape recorder. Personal resistance was felt through the entire session.

We are here speaking from within the silence of your being. We thank you for your effort in communing once again. We wish to speak about manifesting on the Earth Plane of existence. Know that the Earth Plane is one of the intermediary planets on which manifestation *(manifestation being the action of thought upon matter)* has not reached its full potential. Earth is in an intermediary state and its inhabitants have not learned or reached a point where their thinking and desire nature is focused and clear enough to manifest clearly the result of desires.

Manifestation takes place constantly. All that you think and all that is in your life is a replica and mirror of the activity of your thought and the intensity of your emotion and desire nature. Most beings live in massive confusion; one thought counteracting and negating the other. Fear is the predominant atmosphere on your planet and negates the more positive desires.

Earth is like an experimental station. There are other

dimensions where thought is instantaneous, where fear is known as an illusion and does not exist and where the most wondrous events and worlds and universes are experienced through thought alone - instantaneously bringing the created to its creator.

You are creators in your earthly existence and are here attempting to create and manifest joy and love as your challenge. What you agreed and came here to do, to learn. You all seek to be happy. You all seek joyous harmonious lifestyles but many of you are addicted to pain and the lower base emotions to the extent that you do not have a clear feeling of what joy is, of what happiness is, of what lightness is. In order to manifest these they must first be felt within you. Nothing external you reach out for can give this to you.

Most of you go about thinking the acceleration of your finances will bring you the happiness you want. That another human being in relationship will give you the happiness you want. You go chasing something that is not felt within. First it must be felt within without placing conditions for its manifesting. You must throw out of your consciousness all thoughts having to do with pre-planned ideas of what will bring you happiness, what will bring you joy.

As long as you continue to think that the right relationship, the right financial situation, will bring you these you will not receive them no matter how hard you try to manifest them. First you must experience and ask for the highest to manifest in your life. To cut through with the sword of clarity and light. Cut through the illusion, the veil, the hypnosis that you accepted as far as the conditions that will bring you what you seek.

Observe nature. Nature is joyous as it grows and moves

and becomes all that it can be. Observe the animals. They are the pure in heart and in expression. They live from moment to moment from the clear impulses of that which created them and that which dwells within them - the mind and the heart of God. They express themselves honestly. They do not attempt to impress each other. There is no class distinction. They do not run to houses of worship to worship their creator. They worship their creator by simply being what they are. They worship their creator by moving, acting, moment by moment on the impulses within.

To manifest happiness while you have the opportunity, you must come back to yourselves. You must worship within the temple of yourself. You must move and act, moment by moment, following your own internal rhythm. You must love and care for yourselves, be responsible for yourselves.

No external has power over you and yet you give your power outwardly to whoever and whatever appears within your illusory thought to have authority, to have influence, to have opinion of you. You seek and seek and seek so far out from yourselves that you've lost yourselves. You are not present - barely present in interactions with others because your attention is focused on how you are appearing; your own self-consciousness and what you will say next that will be equal, intelligent, accepted. Your thoughts are not upon yourself, honoring yourself. Your thoughts are trying to know what the other person thinks of you and align yourselves with whoever that may be. Giving, once again, an external the power over you. Losing yourselves bit by bit.

This is the time to claim your power back, to be whoever you are. Whatever that is in any way that it wishes to express itself. Rather than express yourself in diminishing ways to please another, learn either brutal honesty, expressing yourself as clearly and as honestly as you possibly can, or be silent. Nothing else is acceptable.

Each time you diminish yourself, each time you move and align yourself into the atmosphere of another who you've given power to, you lose. You lie to your inner self. It is experienced as a lie and confusion is registered within. The more you allow it, the more confusion. The more confusion, the more confusion compounds itself and eventually, you lose yourself.

Very few walking your earth plane can claim honesty. Honesty of self. So very few ever truly know another human being for who and what they truly are. So few can be honest and true to themselves. Self-truth, loving yourself enough to be honest with yourself. In being honest with yourself, you're honest with the world. The masses of humanity are hiding - hiding their true selves. Hiding what and who they are in order to be accepted by a society that is hiding who they are. Your world is in a state of sorrow, fear and hiding.

Watch your animals. Watch your pets. Learn from them. They are truly the guideposts to mirroring what you can become in the context of living freely, living honestly. When you view an animal at any moment your eye and attention touches the animal, you are observing honesty, truthfulness. Whatever it is they are experiencing is being shown outwardly at any moment. Animals cannot deceive. Animals cannot hide what they are experiencing, what they're feeling. Wondrous creatures that they are. Learn from them. They do not judge you or each other. They have no opinion of you. They care not what your race, creed or religion is or what you're wearing or how you're eating. They accept you for whatever you are without a thought of changing you or changing your beliefs to coincide with theirs. Observe your animals and learn from them about unconditional love, about living freely, about simply being.

Transmission 19: November 23, 1987 (Personal)

You have been appointed, in part, for your adventurous spirit and the predominant constant inner thread of intention which seeks truth in all situations. Why think you now your life events have converged as they have and plummeted you into the cauldron of confusion?

The intense call for truth and right action, based on truth, is the cord which strengthens our alignment with you. Your calls are being answered. You must manifest our intention. The confusion will soon clear. Each day brings you closer to the realizations you seek.

Know that the way is being made clear for you to move beyond the walls of your resistance and let our message through. You must stop questioning the validity and the quality of the message and let it shine through. These words will impact many and begin them on a path of inward search for the truth of their own being. Our words are meant to shatter the illusions existing in individual consciousness and experience, and open the doors to the light of truth.

Do not dwell on how you will be received. It is the message, and the forthcoming message, behind and beyond the message, that needs to manifest.

TRANSMISSION 20: NOVEMBER 23, 1987

Spoken into the tape recorder. Telepathic/verbal expression was on a much faster key than usual, giving me little time to think about what was going on or being heard.

Now is the time for us to dictate information that will bring you to a higher level of consciousness.

Loving yourselves is prerequisite in any attempt to consciously achieve a higher state of being on your Earth Plane. Loving yourselves, and the full ramifications of what that encompasses, must be fully ingrained in the consciousness of everyone, if peace is ever to be maintained or experienced either within yourselves or on this earth en mass. Most of you life in states of self-deprecation. Most of you live in states of fear, jealousy, lack of confidence and all the other self-defeating patterns and thoughts that hold you back from experiencing the fullness of your experience on this Earth Plane.

We are here to teach you. We are here to wake you while there is still time. How many lives do you wish to experience going over the same patterns, making minute progress when full enlightenment and realization can be achieved in one lifetime. Very difficult though, at this stage of human soul progression. However the energies available at this time will afford the greater opportunity for this to manifest as we've spoken in prior sessions.

In experiencing self-love, you experience your oneness with God. God is the animating, life-giving force within each of you. To think poorly of yourselves is to think poorly of God.

"I am the spirit of love within each of you. I call you to nurture yourselves and to nurture those who come into your radius. I call you to myself. I am the radiance within you. When you align yourselves with my energy, I am then the radiance that shines forth and emanates from you. I am love. Throughout your lifetime I seek to bring you to the realization that I am present and that we are one. I seek to bring you to the realization that will lift the veil from your memory and enable you to be what you originally were born from. You see, in the beginning you were one with the Creative Force. The All in All. There is no separation. And when the All in All expanded beyond itself and gave birth to itself, you were thrust into the ethers of time and space to continue the creation as part of the Creator. I am here, always myself, leading you back to the conscious realization of your origin. You are a Divine spark. One with the Creator. As you progressed through your sojourn of the soul, you forgot who you are and you forgot that all creation and manifested forms are who you are. All originated and were born from the One. All are parts of yourself. And I move through and have my being in all, equally. When you look upon another human being or another life form, regardless of how it has chosen to manifest its creation, know you are looking upon part of yourself and into the face of God. In the beginning, you were one and still are."

When you're critical of another, you criticize yourself. When you judge another, you judge yourself. When you take from another, you take from yourself. When you hate another, you hate yourself, and your self reacts in kind. When you love and accept another, you love and accept yourself. When you reach out with compassion to another, you comfort yourself. When you reach out to heal another, you heal yourself. When you reach out with enlightenment toward another, you enlighten yourself. All that you do outwardly you do to yourself. All that are in your radius are there because they are part of you - drawn to you and you to them to mirror yourselves, to heal yourselves, to love yourselves.

Do not judge, analyze or criticize another. As you think and do and as you speak the words to express your judgements, your self within hears and believes what you say to be true of *itself* - reinforcing your outer judgements as part of itself, compounding your difficulties, strengthening the bars of your prisons within.

Seek to know others with the loving heart and all encompassing vision of the Creator who judges not, who shines and exists in its totality with all.

Love God

Love yourselves.

Transmission 21: December 9, 1987

———————— ⚜ ————————

Early in the morning, I heard the following:

I am here with you.

I responded mentally: What do you wish to express through me?

We wish to express how human beings can enter into communion with their God selves. Conscious alignment and communion with the God self is the primary purpose for humans on this Earth Plane. When you enter into the realization that there is a multidimensional system taking place within your human system, confusion initially begins to be experienced. Fear begins to be experienced. The cauldron of consciousness stirs. The High or God self begins to prepare itself for its infusion into your conscious mind. It waits in readiness throughout your entire life and through the challenges experienced by the soul. The soul bringing forth the necessary experiences to bring the conscious you to a state of receptivity and readiness.

Crises and challenging situations are the tilling of the mental/emotional soil of consciousness preparing itself for the seeds of the High Self. The God self to be planted in the newly tilled soil. Know that all your experiences are valuable experiences. Do not judge your experiences as 'good,' 'bad,' 'evil,' 'holy.' They're all holy and all bringing you and leading you to the finer path of light, life and creativity.

It can be assumed that if you're listening to these words or reading these pages, when these words become manifest into pages for those to read and experience, that you have entered this life with the intention of service to your world in some way. Think not that your service must be manifest in a grand way or that you must be visible in the public eye. It's those who remain on the home front experiencing their daily lives in their professions, in the world, in their simplicity, who can manifest the higher principles by living them, that touch many and begin the process of higher thought and transformation in those around them. Let yourselves, your lifestyles, be the example. Let your homes and workplaces be your arenas for refining yourselves and manifesting the principles of light.

When the conscious being realizes that there is a path, that there is guidance somewhere within them, that there is a higher vibration, a higher life to align with, it is necessary to enter a listening mode at all times. Alignment means alignment. Alignment means the High Self, the God self is there - present, conscious within you at all times and sharing the life with the other facets, namely, the lower unconscious and conscious minds.

Stating intention can help the listening mode. *Say: I intend to consciously align with and respond only through the impulse of my God Self, my High Self. I know that any words spoken, any actions taken, any decisions made through this level of consciousness will bring me to a higher state, will prevent the forming of new karma and clear the way for me to experience freedom where I can rest within my own being with the knowledge that I am attuned, that I am aligned with the highest, that I am being guided, that I am being nurtured and loved.*

Much of your earthly loneliness will be dispersed and dispelled in the light of this experience. Spiritual loneliness will then manifest where you consciously know that you're reaching upward beyond yourself to make the alignment stronger and stronger, realizing that this is the truly important achievement that can be made during your sojourn on this planet. Your planet is a school to experience and to align consciously with your Creator.

Do not chastise yourselves if you fall from what you think is grace. Do not chastise yourselves when you become angry or jealous or fearful. Those who chastise themselves for these experiences can rest in the knowledge that there has been a pivotal point of realization, that the baser, non-productive emotional responses are not in alignment with the higher order of life.

The awareness of their destructiveness will imbed itself in a greater way, through greater realizations each time they are experienced. The entire being will make the necessary shifts within and strive to transcend and realize the uselessness and the destructiveness. To realize that nothing that can stimulate these responses can really hurt you - the realization of the illusions that are created and the illusions that you respond to and the power that you give others over you. Eventually the barriers will melt away. In these instances, your anger, fears, etc. are catalytic points, catalytic experiences and will become more and more uncomfortable and force you to reach even further within and without for this Grand Alignment to consciously take place.

Your purpose here is not to kill those emotions but to transform them, to transcend them and to let your actions, words and intent become one with the greater awareness. That you may recognize your fears, your angers, what creates dissension within you and in their presence, not react in harmful ways toward yourself or anything or anyone in your radius. To follow the guidance and the path of the greater awareness. To master the emotional self, master the animal self - allowing it to feel. You have not much control over that. Not denying its existence, but taking right action in the face of its assault within you.

We are there as emissaries for the Creative Source. We are akin to the antibodies within your system that dispel disease. We now your trials and your sufferings. We know your confusion. We know the difficulties presented to you on your Earth Plane. We are 'a force of light." We love.

TRANSMISSION 22: DECEMBER 11, 1987

———— ❧ ————

Received early in the morning while having coffee.

We are here.

L ife suspended in motion between the higher and lower selves is what the average human experiences. Hence the confusion. You are constantly existing in the state between two worlds and focused consciously in your earthly reality, thinking it is the primary reality, when the others are, in actuality, more real.

It is only when the inner sight opens to reveal the subtle dimensions of reality that you discover the fullness and the mechanics of the 'game of life.' You create the rules of the game semi-consciously and play semi-consciously until the inner sight opens and reveals the subtle worlds to you. Until this takes place, you walk in a waking sleep state. Pre-requisite is becoming aware of your lower consciousness and your higher consciousness.

We will proceed to give you identifying factors of how to discern which one is in conscious activity in your awareness, so you may respond with conscious awareness and keep focused and moving with the light. The primary purpose being to not accrue additional karma for the soul to magnetize itself irresistibly back into physical form on Earth with its perpetuating struggles. The purpose being to walk and create, consciously in light, with full awareness that you are creators.

The lower self attracts situations and persons to you and bonds with affinities. It serves you by attracting its likeness to you to mirror itself and be recognized. The lower unconscious wants and needs to be recognized. It is like an infant left alone crying for attention and being perceived as an annoyance. The more it is ignored and suppressed, the more dissension is created and the more it wants to express and mirror itself. It reacts to affinities. If there is anger stored within itself it will attract others with like anger which it absorbs and reacts to through your emotional body or, it will attract those externals to stimulate its anger for expression. If guilt is stored, it will attract and lead you into experiencing some form of punishment - separation, loss, physical abuse or illness to satisfy your need to be punished.

If grief or sorrow is being held within, it will attract situations and persons and will construct situations which will offer the opportunity to release your sorrow through tears. All these stored and stagnant emotions are calling for release and expression. They are stored and stagnant because they were not allowed to be expressed to their fullest when the experience that created them occurred. Stored, akin to clamping a hand over a baby's mouth when it seeks expression. This may seem to be oversimplifying a complicated process, but better to oversimplify to get the basic message 'felt' than overcomplicating and engaging the overused intellectual consciousness. These words being put forth will reach the very depths of those who read them with sincere intent in achieving and advancing higher states of awareness and freedom in their life experiences.

The lower unconscious, being part of a primal intelligence, will seek to harm or strike back at any source it perceives as a threat to its safety. When this response is felt within, know it is the lower unconscious. The higher unconscious cannot strike. It is the embodiment of peace and love and knows all external situations and persons are present to further its emerging qualities within you.

The lower unconscious must be taught and subjugated to the higher will through your conscious discipline and control. Do not allow it to strike out in harm, for as you strike, you or those dear to you are stricken in kind. Know this. This is what was meant when it was said to 'fear God.' The universe will mirror and magnetize back to you all your thoughts and actions. Be alert. Be aware. Love God and the God that exists in all.

All experiences of fear are from the lower unconscious. The higher unconscious knows no fear, knows there is nothing to fear. It is the epitome of peace and love and knows that all is well. It fears not death or bodily harm. It lives in the heavenly realms, attuned and one with the Creator of all. So, when fear is experienced in its myriad forms, from anxiety through panic states, you are experiencing the lower unconscious fearful for its survival.

Often, before the infusion of the higher consciousness into one's conscious awareness an intense battle within begins. The human entity experiences the assault of erratic emotions overshadowed predominantly by fear states; states where one seems to be 'coming apart' with no focus for stability. This can be a combined reaction to emotions suppressed, unrecognized, which have been existing in a semi-dormant state of life within, as well as unresolved experiences from past lives which find their opportunity for emergence to be transformed and healed. The more the entity has strayed from expressing their true nature, denying their emotional responses, adapting false masks and facades, the greater the intensity of the experience.Prior to the onset of this Grand Infusion of higher energies, there is usually a crisis situation which forces some aspect of reality to emerge and rip away the veils of illusion which shakes the foundation on which the being built their existence.

Sadly, so many have strayed and stepped aside from their true natures to be accepted by others who are in no better a position. Sadly, so many must go through the painful process of near annihilation to then accept a greater awareness, to realize what is truly important and of value. So many are blind. So many lost on your earthly planet. This is why we have been called and have responded to your call. Our compassion and love stream forth to you and we are here, present, emanating our energies around your globe, infusing those who will receive us.

Another aspect of recognition of the selves is the experience of obsessional love or obsessional sexual attachment when related to physical gratification only. This is of the lower self. Know that sexual engagement can never fulfill itself. Can perpetuate itself into an uncontrollable motivating force in one's life, but no matter how many times you engage in sexual intercourse, even if the opportunity is constant from waking to sleeping, day upon day, this urge will not be fulfilled in the totality you seek. What is truly being sought, unbeknown, is the fusion of spirit to spirit - soul to its Creator - The Sacred Marriage - the infusion of the God self with the human entity to know itself consciously as God.

Many of those aware (your teachers of the East) recognized this and chose to forfeit physical sexual contact and its temporary gratification and temporal pleasure and with consciousness of intent, directed their sexual energies into an upward movement in the search for fusion with God. However, the decision to forfeit physical sexual expression can only be done in a healthy way through the realization of its value and inner direction of each individual. It does no good and can create harm and more suppressed energies to follow the instructions of a teacher or order which insists this be done. It can only be done with the desired outcome of fusion with spirit through one's own evolved inner realization of the process. Give not your body or mind to any one teacher or sect. Keep your own counsel. Love yourself by expressing your self, being your self, and accept no restrictions or limitations from external sources.

TRANSMISSION 23: DECEMBER 21, 1987

—————◦❦◦—————

Received in the morning while having coffee in
response to my question:
What do you wish to express through me?

The knowledge of love. True love, loving as the Creator loves, is allowing, accepting, and acknowledging all life as it is. Putting fears and projections of fears in regard to the 'loved' one aside. The veil of fear projected on to anything negates and dilutes the vibration of love. Unfortunately, most on your planet are not able to penetrate the veils that prevent freedom of love to be experienced. Are not yet able to attune to the Greater Awareness where it is known there is nothing to fear. And so your loves are stifled and fear is experienced more than any love.

Set your loved ones free by allowing them to be whoever and whatever they are. Do not try to change anyone. Everyone is perfect as they are, following their own internal rhythm. If you want to be loved in its true sense, then you must learn to love. To love is simply love and accept a being in its totality, respecting its unique expression and being. The moment you criticize, the moment you are intrusive, the moment you try to change someone else you fall 'out of love' and 'out of respect' for its essence.

The attempt to change anyone else always reflects selfishness on your part, manipulation on your part in some way. The exceptions to this are the true saints and teachers who, in their loving detachment, simply emulate the love of God by being that, and allowing others to experience them as a living example. Otherwise your 'if onlies' and attempts to enlighten those around you are selfish manipulations, expressions of possessiveness and superiority that will always fail and are intended to make you feel better. Set your loved ones free to experience their own expression. Whether it pleases you or not. The moment you can set them free, and love them, you will have your love truly returned.

Think of those in your life who you are truly comfortable with, who you truly love. Are they not the ones with who you can express yourself and be yourself fully and not feel judged or criticized or manipulated, or prove anything to? Think on this and you will know. Who are the ones you withdraw from and why? Are you not withdrawing because you sense their need for you to live up to certain expectations or feel you need to hide certain aspects of yourself? When you need to hide and alter yourself freedom/love is diluted and distorted.

Set your loved ones free from your expectations and you will know love. Conquer and release your own fears. And as you do, be yourself. At any cost, always be yourself. Attend to learning to love yourself first by being yourself. When you can love yourselves, then you can love others truly in the full sense of the word. You see, unless you can achieve self-love you will always be looking to externals to fulfill you and they never can. You will never find peace within yourself because there will always be someone or something in your experience that you will perceive as disappointing you and keep your focus projected onto them as a measuring rod for the extent of happiness you can experience.

'If only' this one would wake up or that one would do this, or be a little more this way, I will feel better. Nonsense! You will never feel better unless those thoughts you project onto others are annihilated from your mind.

Attend to being true to ourselves and accepting all others for who and what they are expressing. Honor them. Respect them. Respect the God within all who rises up within all to help, to guide and to awaken each to its presence. Only when the God within you is externalized and you become it, will you truly know love of yourself, of others, and from others. Yes, this is one of the most difficult lessons on your Earth Plane and the one that creates the highest resistance. And if this is the only truth you learn fully, it is the greatest to be learned. So be it. We thank you and we love you and send our waves of love to shower you.

TRANSMISSION 24: DECEMBER 22, 1987

Received in the morning while having coffee. I began to hear the following words and started writing:

Within each family system an unspoken pact exists. The pact represents the activity of existing children representing various aspects of the emotional patterns and behavior nature of the adult (whether blood children or otherwise) who take on the task of living through the unresolved issues of the parents, as well as their own; bringing the next generation onward to a greater awareness and helping the parents to see parts of themselves and the result of their patterns externalized.

Your children are extensions of yourself. Although each has come to you by their individual choice of soul magnetism and you have drawn them to you in need of a teacher. Your children are your greatest teachers. Your families are your greatest opportunities for reaching enlightenment, the true experience of love, respect for individual soul essence, Divine detachment and freedom. Your children are your mirrors as you have been to your parents and your parents are to you. No random relationships exist anywhere. All are related and are drawn to one another through the magnetic chord of affinity.

As parent, know that you are the vehicles enabling another creative life essence to exist and express itself on your Earth Plane. Each has entered with the seed of the consciousness of God. Each has its own unique internal rhythm and characteristics. Each has entered with a life-plan or intent of evolutionary accomplishment. Each born into this world is a notch greater than the prior generation, having had the opportunity to experience the advances in consciousness of humankind and Earth in its non-physical dimension as well as the genetic advances through the fusing of its own conception. Each is unique and it is this uniqueness that must be honored. Each has chosen you as parent for the qualities and opportunities it knows it needs for its advancement toward fulfilling the soul urge to fuse with the Creative Source.

You might ask: Why would a soul choose to enter a lifetime of pain knowingly?

The soul's perception of your physical world is quite different from the perception of the physical consciousness of reality and encompasses the true reality of what it is. The soul perceives an earthly life with full knowledge that time spent here is merely like the flicker of an eye in the scope of eternity. It views your dimension of Earth as both playground and school.

It responds also to the irresistible attachments that were left unresolved with others as well as the (subconscious) calls from those on Earth who are seeking to fulfill their unresolved experiences. Mutual needs are magnetized.

While in physical consciousness you will never know all your past life experiences and how they affect you presently. You are barely aware of how your thoughts, actions and experiences of this life affect your life pattern now. The most that can be expected from discovering prior life experiences are fragments of awareness that will help you to understand and take responsibility for your current existence, and perhaps resolve or release energy memory blocks which have bearing presently. All will never be known, however, which brings us back to the purpose or initial intent that you all are here to accomplish - which is to consciously align with the God self and live the principles of truth and harmony with all that exists in the present time. This automatically transmutes experiences of Karmic origin and brings you to the point of enlightened existence, freeing you from the irresistible pull to physical existence on Earth.

This does not necessarily mean your challenges cease. They continue for the benefit of further refinement of the soul's experience. No life is random. Each life has its pattern, its rhythm, certain specific tendencies that were chosen to be experienced and refined. The pattern continues through your entire sojourn bringing with it the experiences and situations for further evolving and greater understanding.

Each life form exists with the pattern and vibration of its own growth cycle and the perfect vibration and essence of the universal light-rhythm of ever expansion, evolution and creativity which is akin to a tuning fork. The perfect rhythm is there. The perfect sound to which we all aspire to align with knowingly or unknowingly. Pay attention. Seek the impulse of thought from the higher realms of harmony. Accept and take responsibility for all your experiences. Value all. Release your fears and resentments. Seek the greater awareness which will free you. Listen for the answers to your unspoken questions. We leave you with this.

Transmission 25: January 16, 1988

I asked the question: What is it you wish to express through me? I saw the words 'spirit guides' in my mind's eye. I questioned, wondering whether this was what really wanted to be expressed and I resisted. Then I heard an inner voice say: "Please write, Marina"

We wish to express more about the concept of spiritual guides and past-life experience. Many of what are identified by persons as spirit guides are the whisperings of energy forms that they had inhabited in prior incarnations. These forms, as encapsulated energy, are striving to complete what was left incomplete in the experienced incarnation There is nothing to fear with this knowledge, as all human life is experiencing this. Most of your spirit guides are you; fragments of energy that have not been fused into the Creative Source. Some are related to talents or gifts which were realized and wish to continue to express and evolve. Some have to do with major attitudes and traumas that need to be integrated consciously and resolved.

When a person experiences a fragment of a past life, (as in a regression experience) it is the energy spark of that personality/personage that existed in physical form transmitting the essence of its pattern which is being played out once again in your current focus of existence. You are still one with all these forms. They are part of you - not separate - an integral part of all you are now, from the highest to lowest. So, you carry these energies which are the force of continuing evolution towards wholeness and fusion.

Each human embodied form, focused in physical reality, also has the one great spiritual presence which is part of the Creator - the giver of life. Imagine it as a beam of light from the sun or core light of the universe beaming down and connecting you to its loving presence. The vibration and impulse of the Creator is ever present within each, silently emanating its presence. It is. It exists. It is silent. It simply emanates at all times. It is up to the individual to recognize its presence and flow of thought/impulse.

You, on Earth, cannot be still, cannot find peace or fulfillment until you align with this existing vibratory essence. You will be pushed, prodded, satisfied only temporarily with your achieved goals until this alignment takes place; and then you'll find the simplest form of lifestyle to be the most rewarding. But, don't relinquish your lifestyles in a false attempt to reach this state. The most elaborate of you who relinquish in purity are the highest blessed.

It is when you've achieved and possess all the entrapments of physical/material existence and give them up for the joy of joy and simplicity, that the greatest peace and progress is integrated. It cannot be done backwards by alienating, isolating yourselves first and creating simplicity in the hope of spiritual rewards. That is evasive action.

Many of your greatest spiritual souls with the greatest challenges have come on to Earth to amass fortunes, to create and create and create, fully in the stream of life, and to then surrender all achieved for simplicity. The great souls know this process, or pattern for incarnated choice of a spiritual path. They are here to teach you with that one great act, which most of you do not understand, but never forget. You think they're mad!

Most of you unconsciously fear what you call success which is usually misinterpreted as the achievement of material goals and status within your society's structure. Inwardly you know the ultimate requirement of then giving it away. You fear the loss; and yet, those who struggle the entire lifetime to achieve, and then realize simplicity, give it away joyously. The extent of your inner disturbance hearing this is the extent of your lack of understanding of what true joy and peace is, what true alignment is. We, by no means, advocate poverty. The poverty state is not desirable and is not what is meant by simplicity.

The one church who is steeped in greatest wealth could, of its own decision, give its wealth away in establishing resources to elevate those less fortunate. To establish ways in which they can help themselves. Giving to rescue a temporal situation stands lame in the face of giving to establish teaching foundations for self-reliance. They would become the greatest church who would teach and impact the entire world about loving their brothers and giving.

TRANSMISSION 26: JANUARY 18, 1988

Received while having coffee in the morning. I heard the first few words come in quickly and began to write.

There is a pollyanna attitude existing among many of you who are spiritually inclined with regard to your personal evolution and the evolution and survival of the Earth you inhabit. The predominating illusion is that if you reject and don't think or speak about the possibilities of massive destruction or annihilation, it will not come about. That if you send light across the globe, you are powerful enough to stop what may be looming on your destiny's horizon. You become caught up in the addiction of spiritual pursuit and reach out to others to convert them or to expound your newly acquired awarenesses. You see the lacks in others before acknowledging the very same within yourselves, adapting a false superiority.

You become angry and reject the prophecies given in the past by those gifted with future vision and connectedness to our impulse. We were present then. We have been attempting to enlighten and forewarn your inhabitants for centuries through those gifted souls who had the strength to stand apart and speak their visions out of the mainstream of beliefs, putting their lives at stake for love and truth. Those who could translate our impulse were few and far between. Their numbers have grown through the multiplicity of their genetic structures, being reborn again and again. They are with you now in greater numbers. Their descendants are with you, receiving the same messages of warning to mankind to stop, to lift the veils of their closed minds and see what is happening in your world; a world which was meant for joy and bounty.

You who teach must open your minds to global awareness. You who teach awareness must prod your students to take action for themselves and the world around them. You are the informers. You are the translators. You must let them know that the Earth and its inhabitants are moving swiftly into dangerous waters and that everyone's cooperation is needed at this time to hold back and reverse the tides of annihilation. Your Earth is rebelling against the constant assault of its body and spirit. This can yet be reversed but there are not enough numbers of you presently speaking out or taking action.

The darker forces of the universe, and they do exist, are side by side with us, separated by a very thin veil of dimensional substance - watching, emanating their essence as well. They wait to see the outcome of their own survival. They represent the self-destructive, unenlightened energies which have evolved through the separation in the consciousness of man from God. God has not separated from you. You are always one, but you have forgotten and created the separation.

These dark forces are aware and fear what they perceive as their annihilation if their controlling presence is overpowered. They fear change. They represent your addictions to the baser emotions, the self-destructive, the guilts, perpetuation of fear, control of others. They revel in strong negative experience. They know nothing else. They are addictions to the negative forces of inertia and fear. They do not know another way. They are what they are and they emanate as well. The baser emotions are their nourishment as they need to feel intensely to realize their existence.

And yet, they are also of God. All is of the Creator and we love them with the same intensity as we love you. And you must also love and not reject them or the negativity within yourself. You must encompass all with love and in so doing, darkness will transform and be absorbed into light. Light cannot transform into darkness. Light is all that is, and by its nature, expands itself.

Darkness is resistance, inertia, clinging, static, fearful, compulsive, dense. Feel these qualities within you and see them externalized in your world. When you feel them within you, seek to change the essence of the feeling into flowing, non resistant expansiveness. Break the chains that bind you and your Earth.When you can truly love that which is despicable - when hour heart can reach out to the profane with love and compassion, you will be a light unto this world which will burn eternally. Marina, we thank you. We know this is difficult.

TRANSMISSION 27: JANUARY 20, 1988

———————— ⚜ ————————

Received while having coffee in the morning. Heard the first few words and tried to get away.

There is a new wave of energy vibration weeping across your Earth presently. All life forms are responding to it. It may seem to be as a distant sound that is first sensed in the atmosphere around you with causes you to become silent and emend your senses behold yourself to attune to it. Something in the air. The outpouring breath of God sweeping over its creation. It is akin to a tuning fork resonating a silent sound and all life, including animal, plant and mineral will feel its resonance and unconsciously move towards attunement and a higher way of being. This represents one of the initial stages of the 'Great Awakening' which is in process and progress. Creative evolution is accelerating its movement within all.

You will be called to live the principles of peace, harmony, and right action in your personal lives. You will be called to turn and face yourselves and your patterned thought responses and actions; to make your choices and decisions from the principles of the higher awareness and not the base emotional structures you are presently functioning within. You will be shown in graphic ways the healing that takes place when your choices and reactions (which are choices) are made from higher awareness, and the destruction from your negative patterned responses.

Know that it is difficult to choose the benevolent. Do not be misled into thinking you are, simply because you have acquired a storehouse of spiritual concepts that you can think about and reiterate. It is easy to deceive yourselves and enter your illusory states of false elation and superiority through the knowledge you acquire. You are masters of this.

This is a time for action. Each decision you make (which represents the creative *causal* factors) will have far resonating *effects* in the path of your personal destinies and the destiny of your Earth and inhabitants. Nothing short of impeccable attention and action will suffice. You are leading your planet and its life forms (which depend on you) rapidly into their destiny. The outcome relies on human choice and the framework within which those choices are made. Creative evolution and healing or destruction. Each of you have far reaching impact. Your individual choices resound their effects in far greater ways than you can comprehend.

Never before in the history of your Earth has its fate been more fully in your power. Never before have the polarities of evolution and involution been stronger. Never before has there been the great tension that exists both within the Earth itself and its inhabitants. Never before has the call for survival emanating from Earth been louder. Never before has the resounding response from your Creator (within and without you) been stronger. All is moving into a greater and greater intensity.

You, who are spiritually inclined have the responsibility in your power. Come out of your hiding and speak out. Join with others and fortify yourselves through the power of group or multiple consciousness. This is not a time to be alone in your pursuits. This is a time for unity and refining and strengthening your inner being, intent and purpose. Solitude for the purpose of communion, balance, and learning to know, love, and express yourselves in your own strength and creativity is a sweet balm for the soul. Alienation and isolation through pride and fear breeds inertia and involution.

You who are aware are the mirrors and the leaders/teachers of those who are not. Stay in the world. Allow your presences to touch those of like mind and those who are yet walking with the pack. Allow yourselves to be challenged. Do not fall into states of false superiority. You will only realize yourselves and your imbalances through challenge, not isolation. You will find much of the strength and answers you seek personally through group contact with your spiritual affinities. This is the time for spiritual warriors to emerge and light the way for others.

We leave you now and thank you.

TRANSMISSION 28: FEBRUARY 1, 1988 (PERSONAL)

Marina, it is now important that you begin to realize the full multidimensional nature of your personal existence so that confusion can be dispersed. You are rare in that you are exhibiting the capacity of functioning through many levels succinctly without much fear or inhibiting disturbances. You are progressing with the rapid opening taking place in your being with unusual stability.

The psychic state is related to, but not equal to the channeling state. In your case you have needed to experience the psychic state in order to first be able to synthesize and translate the emanations of individual lives and energies into comprehensive form. This enables both penetration into deeper and deeper facets of yourself and deeper and deeper understanding of the Human Condition reflected by those who your mind penetrates.

With this process, encapsulated in your profession, you have the opportunity to examine many human systems. Now the time is nearing where synthesis of all will be realized. Only through the ongoing use of your psychic perceptual abilities in working with people, has this been availed to your consciousness. Now you are beginning to see how all human life is responsible for life on Earth and you are penetrating the veils of limited perception again, to have the greater realization of how all minds are inexplicably linked and how they create not only their individual futures but the future of your planet.

You have been give this rare opportunity and mental capacity to synthesize and translate for the whole. When we say *synthesize* and *translate,* we mean the capacity to absorb vast amounts of data which emanate from a being's totality (the conscious, subconscious, superconscious, past lives, future lives, physical body, mental, emotional and the external energies represented by persons and environmental conditions in the individual's radius) and penetrate the veils of fragmentation to realize a cohesive order through which you then express your perceptions to them through your language.

Each individual you read for adds to the expansion of this process so that eventually, all types, all patterns, all thoughts, all combinations of human systems and relationships will have touched and been integrated into your awareness, producing the ability to simplify, generalize, and speak for the whole. Simplicity is a great gift. Simplicity and the ability to communicate simply in terms that apply and can be understood by all is the greatest gift you can give. Keep heart. Keep faith. We know how difficult this is for you and appreciate your diligence. You are beyond the point of turning your back now. You must continue with faith and love. Each person you sit with who you touch and open to with your consciousness only deepens your love and intent for the lot of you on your Earth.

The recent upheavals and anguish you've experienced has served you in ways beyond your comprehension; has deepened and expanded your self strongly into yet another dimension, making it possible to channel greater energies and intelligences without fragmenting yourself, which is always a danger for anyone channeling. We are with you constantly and, as you are noticing, our voice is being heard in a more recognizable way

Now, you are leaving your physical form in a waking state more and more and can separate with relative ease. This is not conscious. We feel your fear at hearing this and ask that you step aside from your fear and listen. This process will enable you to reach us more clearly, to receive and retrieve impressions more rapidly and to view the Earth planet from greater vantage points. Also, much protection and healing of others and of yourself is taking place, unbeknown to you.

You have consciously, for years, kept your inner intent disciplined and cleared. You are trusted greatly in our dimension. You know fully the ramifications of ill intent and this will also become one of the areas of proficiency in teaching others. You are a warrior and healer in non-physical dimensions and know this not yet.

Your personal creativity will heighten rapidly, causing much frustration if you do not express. It is imperative that you find a way to express your artistic gifts and bring them into visibility. Seek persons who will take the burdens of daily tasks from you. You must. You must trust.

TRANSMISSION 29: FEBRUARY 5, 1988

Received in response to my question: What do you wish to express through me?

W̲e wish to express the knowledge of hatred. Hatred, who's root is based in fear and separation is like a cancer among those in which it manifests. Where hatred exists there is the absence of faith and love. Fear predominates and the protection and alienation of the self from expanding beyond itself into greater awareness. Hatred prevents expansion. It places its carrier within the tightest of locked prison walls within the human system. To hate is to live locked within yourself. It matters not the source or object of hatred; whether it is focused as prejudice on a race, religion, person, country vs. country.

The most abhorrent hatred is that which hates in the name of the Creator, taking form within the separations of your religious systems. Your religious systems are a mockery of greater awareness and alignment with God. They are one of the greatest catalysts for keeping persons separated from the final step into greater awareness. Most advocate allegiance to the system/church in one form or another and when there is the request for allegiance to anything external, your attention and power is projected onto that external and dependency is placed outside yourself to align with an external system of thought. To step out of their marching rhythm is to then feel guilt. To think for yourself outside the system is to feel guilt, the fear of rejection, and impending punishment that guilt always stimulates. Again, giving power to an external. Keeping masses constricted within a set of man-made laws. Preventing the free expression of one's self through fear of God's punishment. Lying to one's self. Creating separation within and hiding the true self from expressing freely without.

You must all learn to walk alone. You must learn to think for yourselves. Not one system in your world contains the fullness or the reality of truth as it truly exists. Any system you join is limited. Any system or person who gathers people and sets laws is limited. Know this. At the very least, know this.

All contain limitations and distort truth as it exists in the greater reality. And all, because they have walled themselves into a system of thought and laws must, by the very nature of any system, create separation within humanity and false superiority and allegiance. No system on your planet currently has the way for all. The way to God cannot be found within a set of standardized rules and rituals. It is an individualized process by the nature of itself.

God, your Creator, has created all of you and all life. Your life and essence sprang forth from the One Great Soul which is all love. You are all one. Your sun represents your God in that its rays shine on all, encompass all and cares not whether saint or sinner, black or white, Christian or Jew, etc., stands before it. It does not retract its rays from anything or anyone. It encompasses all. You would learn quickly this most simple principle of oneness if the sun, one day, would retract its rays from any one select grouping of individuals.

If Christ were to return to your Earth he would first annihilate the churches and systems organized in his name. Not one represents the freedom and love of his spirit.

I sensed more wanted to be said along these lines but I was interrupted by my dog barking outside and left to let him in. As I returned, the following began and felt stronger than what was being received above and I decided to go with it:

Some of the most dangerous groups to the welfare of humanity are now joining together in silent pockets around your globe. They are not visible yet, but are growing in numbers rapidly and in strength rapidly. As their numbers grow, the hatred which binds them and attracts them to each other magnifies.

We, from this dimension, can only observe. We cannot stop this. We can only emanate our presence and impulse to those who will receive us. We are the informers, the messengers, and we ask you to be aware at all times of any groups, organizations, you join at this time. The highest of them are being infiltrated and your minds are being manipulated in ways beyond your comprehension. There are those countries who are perfecting the art of sending sound waves across the globe, directed to specific locations and persons as a means of manipulation, hypnosis and destruction. There is a silent army of infiltrators ever growing in numbers.

Accept nothing at face value and by what speaks to your ears. You must now develop your instinctual capacities and pay attention to your bodies emotional responses and what they are telling you. Know that there are external forces who are perfecting the art of mass control and manipulation. Their intent is malevolent. Their intent is focused on control of the masses and glorifying themselves. It matters not, at this stage, to identify who and where. Germ warfare is in progress and process.

I'm feeling afraid now but got an impression I'm not completely sure of and that is why I am italicizing this. The impression was that Aids was man-created in a laboratory and that a cure does exist in the hands of those who developed it. Aids is just the beginning. There's more. I'm now questioning whether I am projecting some kind of fantasy or hysteria that I'm not aware of within myself and I ask that I be kept from delusion. Do we ever really know...?

We love you Marina. We are sorry this has to be known. Continue later. Clear yourself now. You are projecting too far into the future of these transmissions and once again, running from your agreed alliance with us.

I am experiencing a need for being anonymous and running and hiding, separating myself from all this. My entire being is torn between the lifestyle I want and the sense of an ancient pact I've made which keeps pushing and shoving and pulling me along these lines.

One month after this transmission, I became ill with a serious case of mononucleosis and could not work for almost a year.

TRANSMISSION 30: NOVEMBER 19, 1988

We wish to express the commonality of all causes. When a person is in the thinking/analyzing stage of creating and the mind is both deliberately and involuntarily straining to reach a desired solution, all the components of creating are called into action..

The subconscious ego nature clings to what is known. It fights for its secure position in what is known, and the set patterns familiar to its existence.

The creative higher evolutionary nature must press forward in its attempt to experience ever new and unfamiliar frontiers, to enable the flow of creation and the evolution and refinement of the being to realize itself as creator. The battle of wills is in process at these points and is taking place almost constantly in the human entity at all times with varying degrees of intensity.

It is imperative in the evolutionary process of the human being to recognize and understand the nature of these two indwelling forces that manifest themselves in a myriad of combinations, but yet remain simply and essentially the same: The forces of evolution and involutional Forward movement and retracting movement, life and death, expansion and constriction, the safety of familiarity and the unknown.

The majority of beings on your planet lean towards the fixed, constricted vibration which, in essence, opposes the natural movement of evolutionary growth. No life, no being, can exist in harmony if it is resisting the force of nature, which is to evolve and grow into all that it can become. You are all irresistibly pulled into ever expansive movement and constant change.

You, who resist what life requires of its very nature, essentially live in constant struggle and imprisonment; limiting your experiences, ever fearful of outcomes and your survival, clinging to what is known as familiar, even as it decays before you.

This planet, Earth, is one of the most propitious environments to realize yourselves as creators and purify and realize your inner intention. Only with mind and spirit working through the density of your physical bodies can you truly realize yourselves as creators. Your environments, the people in your lives, the situations and dramas you find yourselves in, your bodies, all reflect the totality of you to yourselves. All in your radius reflects exactly who and what you are and your current states of being.

All in your radius reflects the current state of your developed abilities to manifest and create. It is important to view your experiences from this vantage point; knowing that you have drawn and created all in your life and all is serving your evolutionary process toward enlightenment.

You are here to create. You are all creators and have sprung forth from the essence of the Great Creator. Your individual lives and experiences, people, etc., are all inclusive in your individual universes which you have created through your attitudes, thoughts, desires, prejudices, limitations, and karma.

View your lives from the perspective of 'individual universes.' Lift yourselves to the point where you can see more and more the broader vision of your created universes. Relentlessly examine your personal (internal and external/ mind and matter) universes and aspire to know the mechanics of how all came into being; whether there is good fortune and expansion or misfortune and limitation. Extend your vision. Seek within to realize the components that brought them into being.

All originates from you and your deepest beliefs; not what you may or may not profess to believe in the facades of your outer world. Your deepest, most hidden beliefs, fears and aspirations.

The journey of life towards freedom begins always within the deepest places within your being. Ask to know yourselves as you are, not as you would like to think you are. Not as you would like to be perceived by others, but as you are.

We leave you now and thank you.

TRANSMISSION 31: AUGUST 13, 1989

———— ❧ ————

Received in the morning while having coffee.

We wish to speak about the folly in holding the thought that you are masters of your destinies on this physical plane. When one speaks of free will, it is generally motivated by the thought of free will to manifest the desire nature on your earth plane. Know that the free will you have, is manifested only on the deeper soul levels and you did enter your incarnations freely and with full and conscious choice through the operation and insight of the wisdom of your deeper self, the soul consciousness, which knows what you need to experience to bring you into conscious communion with itself - the God self. The soul when encased within the human form, is irresistibly drawn to join with its essence, the essence of God.

Each soul has a purpose for being. Each soul has chosen the life, in time and space, that is most propitious for its development and completion. You, as soul, choose the gifts you are to manifest, you choose the limitations you must overcome to become one with the Whole. There is a plan for each of you and each of you have chosen your current existences with all their sorrows, joys and challenges.

We, who speak with you, have experienced and transcended life on your earth plane. We know the hardships and we know the ways of transcendence. We emanate our presence and consciousness as guides to align you with our energies. We are the guides you so earnestly seek, but you must know that we are of one mind, one essence, and that is the essence of God. We are not present to fulfill your desire natures or your temporal wishes, no matter how lofty they may be. We are here and are intensifying our vibration in your lives. We emanate the purity and wisdom of our presence like a blanket over your earth.

Those of you who have consciously called out for enlightenment and freedom will have the greatest challenges. Now is the time for purging and rebuilding. Now is the time for the self-serving, illusory, ego natures to be destroyed. This will be done with each step and action you take, and each thought you think until it becomes crystal clear to you, through the operation of cause and effect in your lives, what is in tune with the vibration of truth, freedom love compassion and selflessness and what is in tune with falsity, temporal desire, separateness, destruction and self-service.

You will no longer be allowed to lie to yourselves; for these are the greatest and gravest lies of all. Complete honesty with yourself is the requirement of this time. Your facades will be shattered.

Deep inward attuning, awareness and examination and purifying your intentions and deeper motivations is what is called for. It is time to look clearly into the mirror of yourselves. You will be challenged. Your self-created facades will fall and those who have funded enough spiritual awareness and power will experience true humility. Out of this will be born empathy and the essence of compassion for the lot of you. True compassion, the forerunner of true love, is the first essential which must establish itself in your planetary vibration in order to free the souls who are still entrapped in your dimension and who will not be able to rise into the height of our dimension.

We can only emanate our consciousness into your dimension. We cannot change world events. We cannot change personal events. We can only emanate the essence and power of the heart of God; and those who are attentive and receptive will be blessed. We are here to help you navigate the shortest route to freedom through the rocky shoals of the troubled waters of your time.

We leave you now and thank you for your attentiveness.

TRANSMISSION 32: SEPTEMBER 23, 1989

———— ❧ ————

The month of October ushers in the beginning of a new cycle of erratic and turbulent energies on your planet. This marks the beginning of the forces which will bring about the 'Great Separation' of souls on your planet. The entire universe is responding to the heightened and erratic energy set into motion last year. All planetary and celestial bodies are about to experience a leap in their evolutionary process with much erratic activity.

Those of you who are consciously spiritualized have the greatest responsibility on the planet; both to yourselves and to those whose lives are still steeped in material reality. You are the teachers and must realize this. Your teaching must be expressed through example in day to day, moment to moment, encounter to encounter. You must live the principles and exhibit the the spiritual wisdom, discrimination and power you have funded. It will take all these components to maintain yourselves and your ideals. You will be tested to the limit of your endurance. This calls for moment to moment, finely tuned awareness.

Your non-physical mentors are closer to you now than ever before as the urgency for victory over the forces of destruction and chaos are reaching unprecedented proportion. You are the bearers of light - the path to follow for your brothers and sisters who are still struggling blindly without the eyes to see higher purpose for existence on this planet.

The past 40 years marked a time of souls incarnating on Earth rapidly and in 'multiple experience' simply to be present for the opportunity to participate in and witness the forthcoming events and be part of the radical change of energies manifesting now.

Many souls have incarnated, without discrimination, in the first available body that would allow entry into physical existence; knowing they would be experiencing unusual hardships with the absence of the ordinary discrimination process prior to incarnation and the absence of their soul affinities while in incarnation. The majority have incarnated with at least three and an average of five other souls attached to them in non-physical form, to experience, integrate and influence the experience of the one primary physical soul's journey.

From time to time and in physically weakened states, the non-physical attached soul personality takes primary control of the entity, causing much confusion in the emotional/mental bodies. On original entry, this is equivalent to a diver leaping into the ocean with several others clinging for the ride.

This phenomena, coupled with the soul fragments attached from past lives, has created much confusion and complexity in your current physical expressions.

There is more influence upon you all from non-physical realms than ever before; both negative and positive. This deems you responsible for the transformation of not only yourselves, but your physical and non-physical brethren.

Transmission 33: October 21, 1989

Received in the morning while having coffee. I heard 'the coming storms' and felt resistance. Then I heard a strong 'write'!

Weather patterns on your planet are going to be dramatically changing over the next five years. This will affect all forms of life on the planet and create higher levels of stress on physical bodies than ever before.

The internal core of the sun is expanding and contracting at a more rapid rate, akin to the pangs of birth, before the rhythm of its new form is manifest. In five years time, a burst of energy in the form of an explosion from the sun's core will disrupt its surface and an unprecedented storm of great magnitude will ensue throughout your solar system.

All life forms will be affected. Extremes of heat and cold, fire and ice. Electrical systems worldwide will be disrupted. In July,1992 there will be the first indication of this phenomena, which is not a phenomena at all, but a natural process of evolution. Radiation will be intense and foreign particles currently protected from entering Earth's atmosphere will be suddenly thrust forth through the protective lawyers which are currently weakening.

The defense systems of most physical bodies will not be prepared to slough off the effects of the intruding elements and a variety of new diseases will manifest. Allergic reactions and respiratory distress will be experienced, skin eruptions, extreme fatigue, confusion and mental aberrations.

Transmission 34: November 15, 1989

We are now going to teach you a new way of being in this world which entails letting go of all structured thought and truly being in the moment. You will be challenged, each step of the way, whenever you attempt to organize your own future based on the people around you and the situations existing.

Those of you who have funded enough spiritual power over the course of your lives will be challenged to live your principles fully, and to distill all the concepts you have pondered into one undeniable truth of life. All thought patterns beliefs and ways of responding which are out of alignment with this distilled truth of life will be challenged in onslaughts of external events and experiences until you come to the full understanding and acceptance of the simplicity of being yourselves and responding, in the moment, through the clear lens of truth, harmlessness, and non-manipulative or controlling action and thought.

Deep, impeccable inner awareness of the higher mind and impulse is necessary at all times and in all your endeavors, speech, action, thought, intention. Meditation on the light and impulse of your higher selves, or known teachers who have reached the purity of enlightenment, is a necessary requirement at this time.

The dimensional substance separating the physical from non-physical realms is ever thinning and blending into one great universe. You will be influenced now from non-physical realms from the highest to the lowest and must curtail your baser instinctual responses with your ever discriminating minds focused on light, truth and the forces of higher evolution.

The greatest challenges are here now. Your planet and its beings have been in endless preparation for this time of radical change and quickening of all vibratory essences. Notice first the seeming contradictions and opposite polarities in the current situations and relationships you encounter on your paths.

And now, you must begin to view your lives truly as paths; paths leading to light and freedom of being - ever moving and changing scenarios, as you tread step by step towards your soul's deeper goal of enlightenment, simplicity and oneness with the impulse of God.

And step by step it will be. There are no short routes to impeccable living and thought. This is what you are here to manifest. Each time you step out of alignment you will be shown in graphic ways, both from your internal experiences and external experiences where the imbalance has occurred, until you grasp the simplicity of it all. You, who do, will become the greatest servants for your brethren.

There is no room or patience left now for pollyanna thinking regarding your spiritual evolvement. This is a time for each soul to grasp the great responsibility for life on this planet. To put it in understandable terms, it is as if God has reached the point of utter impatience with the frivolity superficiality, materialism and bondage existing, and is now bearing down on all life as the Great Father, disciplinarian and teacher.

You all cry for the experience of love, but only a minute few can even comprehend the meaning of love. Your loves stand as perversions of control, clinging, fear and manipulation - expecting others, those you say you love and who love you to pacify and give to you what you haven't had the courage to develop within yourselves - to fill your voids.

You will continue in your endless loneliness, with only temporary reprieves, until you finally learn the fullness and the beauty of loving another in freedom, unconditionally, and without restraints. You will never know love until you can accept another human being fully, as they are, and honor their essence without attempting to create them into replicas of yourselves, who stand justifying your own inadequacies, expecting others to fulfill your needs and take responsibility for your lives and happiness. You have perverted the greatest gift of all - the purity of love, and all is in chaos as a result. The greatest gift you can give, the greatest service you can give, is to accept another human being fully, as they are; love them and also be willing to let them go. Your healings would then be instantaneous and the enlightenment you seek would be yours.

TRANSMISSION 35: MARCH 28, 1990

❧

We are here breathing our essence through you once again. We wish to speak of the entrapments that beings find themselves in and offer ways to inner freedom and peace of being.

Most persons live behind the smoky glass of the facades they have adapted; the face and presence that is projected out into the world which has nothing to do with the reality experienced within the deeper stratum of their beings. Most persons are split between who and what they really are and the outer image and belief system they have adapted which they believe will be most accepted in the outside world. Most have come to believe the facade is the reality and this is where the great tragedy of the human condition lies.

Facade after facade attempting to communicate and be accepted by the facades they encounter in others. Facades communicating with facades, while the essential being lies fearfully hiding its true expression, afraid of revealing its true nature, in dread of being exposed and vulnerable. The underlying thought being: If I reveal my true nature, who I really am and want, how I truly feel, I will reveal my weaknesses. If I am challenged in these areas, I will be noting. Better to hide and keep safe.

In this safety lies self enslavement, alienation, separation and the ultimate loneliness. The tragedy is multiple and exists in the facade and perpetual hiding. Over time, the belief in the facade as the reality and eventually, the loss of contact with one's essential nature.

Most of you are walking your earth fearful of being revealed, even to yourselves. This holds true even when one enters into a psychotherapeutic relationship. It is usually over much time and great courage that the deeper thoughts, fears and truths of one's nature are able to be touched or admitted to. Throughout much of the relationship, the awareness of hiding, protecting and minimizing the truth of oneself and deeper thought is present - even as it continually surfaces within one's consciousness to be recognized and freed.

It is imperative at this stage of current human evolution and existence on your earth that you, who are striving for spiritual consciousness and awakening (you are the leaders and pattern setters for those who are still asleep) begin the grueling task of acknowledging, with brutal honesty, the hidden, dark side of your natures and impulses. Only when a channel within you begins to open and to release and acknowledge your deeper repressions and suppressions can the window to healing yourselves and the planet be opened.

You must acknowledge what is present within you to begin the process of releasing the trapped energies of negativity which prevent freedom and lightness of being. It is not enough to be well read. It is not enough to act through the facade of spiritual consciousness even if your actions and speech have become impeccable in living the principles you've adapted and creating your temporary states of spiritual euphoria or reaching out to teach and 'save' others 'less aware.'

Of major importance at this time is brutally acknowledging your darker impulses and allowing consciousness of them to enter your minds so the trapped energies can be transformed and the deeper levels of the 'human condition' can be experienced by more of you who have awakened. Only then can the new and more effective therapies of transformation and healing be discovered through the consciousness of those healers on the planet who are dedicated to healing your species.

Transmission 36: April 23, 1990

Come to your Father as a child comes for comfort and protection. Speak your fears and burdens directly to Him from the deepest, most reverent place within your being. Then, rest in his love.

Do not pray by rote. Your prayers will not be heard. Pray, each word, each thought, with great reverence from your soul. Learn true communion; soul and heart communing directly with your Creator. Only then will you be heard. Only then will you be answered.

Forgive yourself first before attempting to forgive another. Only then will you know freedom.

Pray that you respond from the voice and impulse of God with in you. Pray for the courage to follow its promptings.

TRANSMISSION 37: APRIL 27, 1990

W̲e wish to express. We wish to communicate information concerning the reincarnation of the Great One who is to be the next Lord of your planet.

There is an entity who will make an appearance in physical form within a period of two years. His essence is not singular, but a convergence of great masters who have lived at one time on your earth. There will be much confusion around his identity. Disciples will perceive the masters they have identified and merged their spirits with. Many will be saying he is the incarnation of this one or that one and all will be correct. He is the embodiment of many and will reawaken and initiate masses of you into a higher consciousness. He will travel worldwide. His feet and presence must touch all corners of the Earth in physical form. Only in physical form can his power elevate those who are drawn to him and also transform the powers of darkness.

As the powers of darkness accelerate their impulse in your present time, it is becoming difficult for the powers of light to reach and influence your minds and hearts to create the bonding necessary for true communion with God and the higher spiritual impulses.

There are too many distractions. Too many individuals personalizing their spiritual teachings and bringing them into the material realms. Your New Age Movement has turned a sad corner and is creating confusion, separation, and disarray. Too much is being sold. Too many inept enthusiasts are leaping prematurely into public view with whatever path to enlightenment or healing they offer and fall into the trap of commercialization and business consciousness.

Few have aligned their minds, hearts, and intentions with the Great Spiritual Heart and are unable to impart true inspiration necessary to elevate the souls they attempt to heal and teach. They function through false spiritual euphoria and are missing the truth they seek to impart. They stand with their egos before them, confident that they are true servants, and blame the opposing forces when their projects and business intentions do not succeed. In most instances, it is the forces of light attempting to enlighten and bring the reality of their situation to them; attempting to avert the growing confusion within the masses.

We urge you to seek out the simple souls who inspire; the simple teachings and books that elevate your spirit with the simplicity of their words and teachings.

The new Lord will bring simplicity. The new Lord will be present and able to impart the secrets and the essence of the spiritual path in one appearance. His feet will touch all lands but once and then he will be gone.

Keep vigil. Seek simplicity. Avoid methods that clutter the mind and inhibit the simple truths. Open your spirit and heart as a child so that you may be blessed and recognize him.

TRANSMISSION 38: SEPTEMBER 2, 1990

W e are here. We wish you to be aware of the struggles you will all be experiencing in this current time. There has been a major shifting of energies affecting your planet.

Old encrusted ideas and forms are now being shattered and challenged. This applies to your Earth itself, your bodies and your emotional/mental systems. It is akin to volcanic activity and eruption. Natural and unseen forces are at work. All that has become crystallized and unmoving will be shattered to make way for the new and revolutionary changes necessary to bring your planet and its beings to a higher state of evolution. You will experience more challenging situations from internal and external origin that will relentlessly force you to become acutely aware of what no longer serves your existence in a forward moving, creative way. All that is not serving your lives or your planet in a positive way will be magnified, shattered, and stripped away.

Chaos is in the wind. The breath of God is sweeping across all creation in a final attempt to awaken life forms to its greater will. The forces of radical destruction and reconstruction are present.

Do not resist by attempting to cling to what no longer

serves you or enslaves your spirit. The more you resist, the more you cling to your false securities, the greater the tension will mount and the greater the chaos will result. This is the time for enforced awareness and experiences.

The breath of God is sweeping away all that does not serve its creation. The reaping of your actions and reactions, both positive and negative, will be magnified. The result of your actions and reactions motivated by fear, clinging, greed, control, inertia, manipulation for self-serving ends, will fall in on themselves and be destroyed. Your actions and reactions motivated by discriminating wisdom for the highest good will flourish. All will reap their harvest through the unexpected, the unpredictable. This, being the action of Karma, condensing its activity in time and space.

You see, you are all here, inherently as creators, to further the creation through the will of God; each in your own unique ways. By the rapid magnification of Karma, which is 'creative law,' you will have greater opportunity to awaken to the knowledge of your essence as creators of your personal existence and co-creators in the fate of your planet.

Nothing is unfair. Nothing is unjust. All life is under the Karmic Law of cause and effect. Not one of you are victims of anything. All in your life, all in your world is the result of the entirety of your incarnations, your thoughts, your intentions and actions. You have chosen and magnetized into your current existences by Karmic Law.

Many souls will be leaving the planet more suddenly and unexpectedly the moment their states of evolution have reached the point of either deadlock, where no further creative activity or realizations are possible; or those who have reached self-realization as creators and choose to leave for a future incarnation of greater service, or to guide from the non-physical dimensions, or to allow entry for another soul struggling for the opportunity of physical existence and enlightenment.

Vast numbers of souls are awaiting entry. The next five years will bring the births of the souls of the extremes. The highest and the lowest will be reincarnating into your Earth for the final battle. Never before have the extremes of light and dark been present in this way at any one time in history. This is truly the most opportune time for conscious enlightenment and completion.

Be aware. Be relentlessly and brutally honest with yourselves. Master your darker natures. Master the art of benevolent choice. Remain harmless. Become powerful. Express yourselves. Master the art of flexibility. Adapt moment to moment. Remain simple. Stay clear and listen for the voice of God within you.

TRANSMISSION 39: SEPTEMBER 19, 1990

A radical shifting of energies affecting life on your planet took place in November 1989. The ushering out of a cycle of order and the sweeping in of a new cycle which speaks of disorder.

The streams/bands of energy from planetary and cosmic forces affecting the Earth and its inhabitants have taken on the quality of condensing and intensifying their energies and effects in time and space. This will be affecting humanity in a number of ways and in all the energy systems of the being. This includes physical bodies, emotional and thought systems and the causal and effect systems you are under the domain of. All systems are under the great stress of intense and rapid change.

Each life system is either operating primarily towards forward movement, order, life and creativity, or towards inertia, stagnation, chaos and death. Imagine a dividing line. On one side is life and all its attributes and on the other, the pull towards death. At any given time, you are on one side or the other, or on the dividing line about to move into one or the other.

There is constant movement and change within all systems of life as the Great Pendulum swings. It is important to become consciously aware of its movement within you and attune yourselves and respect its movement. To fight at the wrong time is to exhaust your resources of life. To be fearful of forward movement and change as the pendulum swings toward life, is equally debilitating.

Each life system has its own rhythm of birth, growth, fruition, death and rebirth. These cycles repeat themselves many times in your lives. This you have no choice in. These cycles manifest whether you like it or not. Not all can move forward consistently in one direction without experiencing the balancing action of the pendulum when it begins its opposite movement.

Life is constant movement, constant change, inescapable change. Those who cling to situations and resist the movement of these changes towards dissolving what no longer serves the higher life of the soul, have the most difficult time of all. Life is endurance and the willingness to endure the movement and cycles of our life path with willingness, awareness, and with grace.

You must remember, and hold in your consciousness, that you have entered this life with the intention of completing yourselves as sovereign beings. With the intention of becoming all that you can be and simultaneously balancing your karmic experiences. You must remember that each lifetime holds the opportunity for completion and freedom for the soul entrapped within the density of your bodies and the tenaciousness of your egos, which cling to the temporal and transient desire states inherent in physical existence. You must remember that when you are about to reach your peaks of creativity, the opposing universal force of the Great Pendulum is ever present to challenge your higher intention, to refine and strentgthen your will-to-good and also to destroy your creations to allow the influence of new energies to manifest in new creative ways. Your creativity and will-to-good will ever be challenged while you are alive.

You must be willing to endure many deaths while in physical form. This is the requirement of the soul. To create, to destroy, and to create again, in every aspect of your lives.

TRANSMISSION 40: DECEMBER 8, 1990

———— ❧ ————

I heard the words, "waiting on the Lord" whispered
and then:

The time has come for us to express to you a way of being that will free the deepest levels of fear and limitation if it is put into practice.

When finding yourselves in despairing states, know that the activity of God is present; magnifying your fears and insecurities for you to become consciously aware of the areas of your life that are yet in fearsome states. Your despairing states are the times when old patterns and fears rise to the surface of your consciousness to be seen and released through faith. The times when what no longer serves your soul's development is released from your life.

There is always the quality of loss, or fear of loss, in any of these states. Know that you can lose nothing. Know that what is being called for is the willingness to acknowledge the transient nature of your world, in which nothing is permanent, nothing is fixed - nothing! Not even your next breath is guaranteed, and then, the willingness to let go and release the idea or situation you are clinging to with in fear.

State to yourselves: "I acknowledge the impermanency of all things; even my physical body. I acknowledge my essence as spirit. I acknowledge the futility of grasping and clinging to what is impermanent and transient. I give thanks for what has been received as life experience from it. I am willing to allow it to pass through my life now. I am willing to remain seemingly empty and void for a time. I know, if I wait, the universe will bring to me whatever I need to continue with the highest level of unfoldment in tune with my soul's intention. I am willing to wait, in faith, resting in the knowledge that God's timing is perfect and will bring to me what I need, not a moment too early, nor a moment too late."

What so many of you do, who live on the constant edge of fear and clinging, is cling to the lesser of two evils; compromising your life's experience constantly. Grasping, groping for a security that is not possible in your temporal earthly existence.

Know that nothing is ever lost. Nothing was ever your ownership to begin with. Not your children, husbands, wives, lovers, material possessions. You own nothing. You are in each other's mutual care; to experience, to give, to receive, to care for.

Everything in your world has a life cycle and rhythm of its own. When it comes into your life (whether person, idea, situation, material possession) it is there for mutual service and because its rhythm corresponds with your own for a time, enabling you to be together. When either's rhythm begins to change and you can no longer serve each other, it will leave your life to make space for the next and greater experience.

Imagine if all the persons, all situations, all material

possessions, all the ideas you have ever experienced were in your life now simultaneously. Do you shudder at this thought? And well that you do!

We implore you to develop faith in the goodness and the perfect expression of the love of God for you. Only as your faith grows, will you be able to release your fears and grasping and live in freedom; knowing that your Lord is ever present and goes before you to prepare the way. But you must be willing to see through the eyes of the Greater Awareness, and through the illusions of your temporal reality. You must be willing to open to the knowledge of the futility of many of your earthly desires and clinging. You must learn to let go and wait, with faith.

TRANSMISSION 41: JANUARY 13, 1991

———— ⚜ ————

Take charge of your lives now or others will. As the energies affecting your planet increase in intensity, the authoritative, aggressive and controlling forces will begin to emerge in a stronger way - both within and outside of yourselves. The battle of opposite forces continues to wage war on your planet and the weaker, non-disciplined, unfocused, will be in danger of being overpowered by the stronger, more organized forces of control and power.

Think not that your lives are guaranteed to continue in a free state of being. As the masses begin to experience more fear and hardship economically, as your bodies continue to be assaulted and worn down in the stresses to maintain your lifestyles of survival, and the gradual poisonings from foods and environment, a generally weakened state exists among the masses of you. Defenses are being worn thin leaving you open and vulnerable to a stronger authority who promises an easier, more affluent way of life.

Know that there are plans in higher secret sections of your government planning a take-over of your country. Know that there is a higher secret world government with a plan for the next 25 years to come into total authoritative power over all people.

The forces of control are gaining in strength as the general populations run blindly unaware of a deliberate plan to seize control on a massive scale. You are being prepared to become a planet of automatons, conceding to and controlled by a stronger, impeccably organized controlling force.

You have allowed yourselves to be distracted by the external material world with its hypnosis and seductions. Each day that passes, more of the will of the individual lessens and will reach the point where you will welcome a government that promises an easier way of life with open arms - making the fatal error which will seal your fates to the authority and will of a handful of madmen.

Think not that your government is protecting you or has your best interest as their priority. You are all being manipulated, weakened of will, and prepared to receive a greater controlling power who will promise peace and ease of lifestyle.

TRANSMISSION 42: JANUARY 15, 1991

W e speak to those of you who are consciously spiritualizing your lives. The challenges for you will be the greatest, as you will have a broader scope of vision and your mental/emotional bodies will be responding to a much greater range of experience than the average person.

As the chaotic aspects of this time increase, you are being called upon to exert your spiritual wills in ever stronger ways. The forces prominent now are not supporting spiritual energies. The 'dark night of the soul,' rather than being individualized, is enveloping your planet. It requires the consistent effort of each of you to put into practice all you have learned and to tenaciously follow the inner promptings which speak of choosing and acting on the impulses of benevolence for yourselves, forward movement, and service to others.

The stronger force will be exerting its influence as a harness to hold back and pull you into states of delay and inertia. You will feel as if you are walking against the wind in your daily pursuits. The persistence of each of you is necessary if a higher order is ever to be established on your planet.

This is the time of testing your spiritual strengths. It is easy to believe and feel spiritualized when all is going well.

But it is during the times of opposition and difficulty that whatever you have accepted and conceptualized as spiritual principle, must be put into action in your daily lives.

Many are called, and the few chosen are the ones who consciously and deliberately move, act, respond, and make their life's decisions based on the higher impulse, in the face of opposing influences. This is the test of this time and it will be very confusing for the majority of you.

It is essential to maintain as optimum a state of physical health as possible. Pay close attention to your bodies, for they are the barometers which reflect your state of being and your vehicle for expression in this dimension.

Seek to maintain optimum levels of energy and flexibility. Consciously seek to counteract the forces of constriction that are affecting you in ever greater ways. This is the time for conscious, deliberate, persistent effort. Listen carefully to your bodies and become in tune with your natural rhythms.

Your bodies reign as ruler, and will surely and silently rebel when consistently forced to endure situations that go beyond the limits of their capacity. Or, when consistently subjected to being in situations they do not wish to be in.

Your bodies will signal you through internal sensations of resistance, constriction, repulsion, and pulling back or, sparking you forward with energy and sensations of openness and enthusiasm. Listen carefully to your bodies signals and how you respond to all facets of your daily experience so that you many become aware of what is giving you energy and what is depleting you. Over time, if the constricting energies are overpowering the energies of expansion, some form of illness or weakening of your system is unavoidable.

If you cannot change the situations you are in, attempt to change your attitude towards them so the body chemistry can alter as well and cooperate in a more positive way. Whenever you can, let go of what you know is weakening you.

Employ a form of conscious spiritual practice daily as nourishment to keep you aligned and open to the higher impulses which are ever present to assist you with your lives. Keep your bodies in tune with a physical practice which speaks of flexibility and heightening energies. Be aware of the interplay of opposing forces, but stay focused and navigate your lives along the higher spiritual impulse.

TRANSMISSION 43: SEPTEMBER 11, 1991

———————— ❧ ————————

We are here, breathing our essence through you once again. We wish to express what each individual can do now to bring themselves, independently, to a greater awareness of the Supreme Power of the All Good and All Mighty within.

You must know in your conscious awareness that you are an inseparable facet of God. That all that is, is within you. This has been spoken of through the ages, but few truly comprehend, parrot the words, teach, but have not experienced the fullness of what this means.

It is difficult for us, in our dimension, to continue to emanate our essence and truth to the current stream of minds that are so cluttered with methods, concepts and parroting what has not been experienced. Few are living the principles they teach and fewer yet, fully understand. There is exhaustion among your race of mankind.

What we wish to convey is the utmost in simplicity - the essence of love and creativity, the essence of becoming all you can become in your life span. But, you cannot do this alone. You must become fully aware and keep in your consciousness that you are the essence of God. That your thoughts have power.

Rampant limitation exists in most of you. Pray to move beyond your limited individual self-created universes into the larger life. Pray to know you are unlimited. Pray to know the bounty of this Earth is yours to share and partake of.

Enter your inner chambers in utmost silence and utmost reverence and realize your oneness with all that exists. Know yourselves to be creators. Know when you enter into the silence of your self, you commune with your creator. When the mind is still, you are one.

You travel to your sacred shrines over the world and the most sacred, the only sacred meeting place is the one within the silence of your being. This is where the holy waters flow and heal. This is where the breath of God embraces you. This is what we have been attempting to convey from the beginning. The more you reach out, the more you stray. Go within. First and foremost, go within the sacred temple of your individual beings and rest in the love of God. Go within so 'He' can guide you and infuse you with his will-made-conscious.

You desire your miracles? You want your guidance? You want your next step? You want to break free? Let us show you how. The way is to experience the direct activity and movement of God in your lives so it is indelibly etched in your consciousness.

Put all pre-planned methods and ideas to rest. Experiment for one month and you will begin to comprehend. Only when you experience the direct action of God will you understand the way of the Most Creative. Will you understand how the 'crooked places are untangled and made straight,' will you understand how 'he goes before you to prepare the way.'

Sit quietly in silence. Ask to know the presence of God, consciously, with all your heart. Ask to be led into the Great Silence within you and be there. Be courageous enough to let your worries and sufferings depart. Let them go. Ask to trust. Be still. In silence.

TRANSMISSION 44: SEPTEMBER 20, 1991

We are here with you. As the current progression takes place in your human systems, it is ever more important to regulate your individual energy systems through some form of silent meditation. Time during each day must be spent in the deliberate act of entering into yourselves, in silence, with the intention of withdrawal into the embrace of the Holy One within and simply being there, present, in the moment, realizing your unity with all that is.

In these times we will be with you. In these times, you are visible and accessible. An open emptied, vehicle is the one able to receive and be infused with the clear waters of life.

Into The Presence

Sitting quietly.
Simply being.
Watching the breath.
Acknowledging the pulse of life within all.
Realizing its presence within you.
Dissolving into your essence.
Aware of the Great Presence moving you into deep all embracing silence.
In silence

God speaks to you in silence.
Simply be.
No past.
No future.
Simply be, now in this moment, with God.

And if 'He' spoke, the words would be...

I am here with you.
Always present.
I am the one you long for and seek endlessly outside yourself.
Be with me now.
I am here with you, now, in this moment.
My love embraces you, as I call you to myself.
I am here with you.
Know this and rest in my love.

Transmission 45: October 10, 1991

In times to come, you will know the presence of the Lord as your life giving power. Above and beyond all else it is important that you now know that the hand and voice of God is among you.

For those whose will has even partially turned to surrender to the will of God, your lessons and lives will be pulled as a river rushing to the ocean, where all, one day, will join in the great sea of infinite love and be drawn back by the sun to your source.

Fear not in times of earthly troubles, challenges, and oppression. You are being guided to the awareness that all that exists as earthly challenge, leads you always beyond the temporal to the infinite.

Your teacher, your Lord, is here with you; present in each moment, ever present, teaching, prodding, probing. The souls of those on earth are being quickened to burst forth anew from within and express the intention and purpose of the Great One.

Chaos may reign in your lives and in your world. You are to hold fast to the spiritual truths that have sparked you, rang true, cleansed and lifted your spirits at the time they entered. Hold fast to the remembrance when you experienced yourselves as one with your Creator. Those hearing these words or reading these words have, if only once, experienced the knowing that they are one with the source and giver of all life. Now is the time to remember. Now is the time to cast away all earthly clinging and ideas that are not in tempo with the higher will. Discipline the mind to remember and your lives will unfold as beautiful flowers before you.

Fear not. Let not the shadows of darkness and temptation pull you further into the dense material world of false comforts. No earthly comfort is everlasting and all can be stripped away in a moment. Join in the great adventure of navigating your lives with the impulse of the Great Force Of Light that surges within you.

Listen with great care, that you may respond to the voice of truth within your being. You will know what is right the moment it is given. Trust and know you are more strongly guided now than ever before. The spirit and voice of the Great Teacher is among you. All of you. Not one of you breathes alone.

You will be challenged to consciously choose, in each moment, the path of truth and the path that will ultimately free your souls from the entrapments of this physical dimension. You will know, in each moment, the way that will move you toward freedom. Courage and willingness to respond to the higher life and to the impulse and guidance given the moment it is given is your task. This will not be easy, as it speaks of constantly facing the unknown.

Your patterned, familiar ways, familiar responses, familiar ways of thinking, create a false net of safety or surety around you. You can be assured of their outcome, even if the outcome is one which leads you continuously to familiar pain or frustration. You are creatures of habit and creatures who cling to what is familiar.

You have not known freedom in your lives and fear it. Freedom speaks always of the unknown and you fear the unknown. You ask for freedom but compute freedom as security in your material, physical, existences and will never know freedom if you continue to cling to this one basic permeating thought. Freedom has no attachment. Freedom has no fear. Freedom does not cling. Freedom does not hide or protect itself. Freedom is visible and invisible simultaneously. Freedom is flight and spontaneous movement.

We implore you to be courageous and follow the higher impulse. We implore you to leap willingly into the unknown. Only in this way can you free your souls' striving towards the freedom of existence. Only in this way can you begin to know the movement and manifestation of God, consciously in your lives.

Choose the unfamiliar. Choose the higher impulse. Embrace the chaos this will initially create in your emotional and mental bodies and move with it, moment to moment. Embrace the unknown, the unfamiliar, and trust. Trust you are being guided. Trust that you know. Trust the Highest of the High is with you in each moment and will make its presence known to you at the most opportune times for you to choose, in the moment, the way to freedom.

Keep courage. You are loved. You are watched over with great care. You can trust.

PART TWO

THE VOICE OF SILENCE

In the Healing Circle

These transmissions were received during the Healing Circle meditation which closed a weekly intuitive development, spiritual awareness group I was leading.

The difference between these communications and the ones in the main text are that they were directed to the persons present in the group and conveyed directly verbally.

HEALING TRANSMISSION 1: AUGUST 21, 1986

Know that those in this lifetime who have hurt you the most, your enemies, if you think of them as your enemies, your antagonists, your tyrants, are your greatest teachers and catalysts in your life to free you. It doesn't matter who they are, what they did to you, the circumstances, or how horrible or painful. Know that if you continue to bind yourself to them, you'll continue to be entrapped. You're not meant to be entrapped. Freedom is your birthright. Love is your birthright. Clarity and happiness is your birthright. But you cling. The pain is in the past. It existed in the past. But yet you remember. You use your minds searching the past, reawakening feelings of pain and not only experience it like the first time, but continue to do it. It is ridiculous!

Your enemies, your adversaries, your antagonists, whoever they may be, also have the essence of God within them. As long as you cling to them, they must cling to you, and neither of you will be free. You keep a negative dark cord attached between. you.

Now, take one person who has been the greatest source of pain in our life. Bring them into your inner vision for a moment or two. Remain as detached as you possibly can and just observe them. Allow yourself to enter their heart and know them. Know their heart and know their experience in a way you haven't allowed yourself to before. See yourselves engulfed in light. Allow the other person to leave in peace. Let them go. Over time, this will free you.

Take in several deep breaths and clear yourself, your mind, body, spirit. Clear your totality and allow the spirit of freedom and light to enter you. Know that you not only helped to free yourself, but helped to free your children, family, everyone in your radius, humanity. Whenever entrapment is transformed, more enlightenment and freedom is returned to the sea of consciousness displacing negativity, limitedness, hatred and grief. Everyone benefits. That's magic!

HEALING TRANSMISSION 2: AUGUST 28, 1986

Visualize a great light streaming from the heart, the mind, and the essence of God - expanding and expanding as it moves. Engulfing you, moving through your being, clearing and cleansing. Bringing you to itself. Bringing itself to you. The movement of yourself reaching to God and God's movement and expansion from within yourself.

Know that the greatest healing takes place in silence, when the mind and body are still and in communion with God. Know that mental gymnastics are never necessary. A simple intent a simple and pure mind and simple heart are all that is necessary. Purity of heart, motive and intent creates within you a natural healer. When you've achieved that, you are the expression of God, and without external physical reaching out, your very presence heals.

I call upon the spirit of Christ to be present. I call forth and evoke the healer within you to emerge. I call forth the God consciousness within you to burst forth and become you, totally, and that you recognize the voice of God within yourself. See God in everything and everyone, regardless of the outer condition, regardless of the appearance. Know that appearance is always deceiving, but know that God is in everything and everyone. Look through those eyes. Feel through those feelings. Know through that knowingness and hear with those ears. Your life will then be free and everything and every one around you will be touched.

You are all loved by this unfathomable presence. Allow it to be known in your being. Rise above your pettiness. Rise above your limitations. Rise above what you think love is and what love isn't. Begin to think in terms of loving everyone. Think in these terms and eventually it must come about. Only then will you be free.

Accept yourself. Stop looking outside yourself for confirmation of yourself. Find who you are. Find your gift and allow it to be expressed through you. You are all channels of energy. You all have your uniqueness.

HEALING TRANSMISSION 3:
SEPTEMBER 11, 1986

K now that you create your future. You create your life. You pattern your entire existence through your emotions, your thoughts, your images and your desires. In order to transform your life into a positive, forward moving experience, you need to become very very aware and observe yourself, the desires you have, the words you speak, and the words, thoughts and concepts you hold about yourself.

You are your complete programming system. Whatever you think of yourself will become a reality and will stay with you to bless you or haunt you. Only you have the power to change that - through the mind, through changing the thought, through becoming aware of your words, actions, feelings and desires. Constant observation of the self. Only you can open the door to light, the door to freedom, the door to happiness.

You want to be happy. You want to have joy. You want to have love. You want to have peace. Whenever you have it, do you fear it is going to be taken away from you? Do you put fear in front of you to adulterate the present? Do you meet a new relationship, or person, or friend, and instead of experiencing the person for who they are, do you keep bringing up past experiences (that have nothing to do with the present person) and through all those fears, project them on to the new situation, creating destruction, worry, fear? Fear, the Great Destroyer.

For the next few moments, give yourselves permission to think about - not the past joys that you've had, not the past happiness you've had, but what you want for yourself now. Not the future. Now! We don't know if we have a future. And before you start, I call forth from within you and from without, the spirit, the essence, the heart of love of happiness, of joyous existence, fearless existence.

Allow yourself now to think and imagine. Ask yourself: What will give me joy? You want to create a lifestyle and a life that will give you joy. Allow your deeper self to show you what you really want. Forget the conditions for the period of time that exists now, in the present, and allow yourself to create. We're calling upon what will give us joy. Many of you don't know what will give you joy. Ask, and allow the answer to come. What will give me joy? Place yourself in the perfect environment - freedom, joy, peace and love, create now.

HEALING TRANSMISSION 4:
OCTOBER 2, 1986

What we wish to speak of tonight is the importance of knowing yourselves; being truly honest with yourselves. Not denying, not pushing into the wastebasket, not saying they don't exist - those negative impulses you have; your jealousies, insecurities, your anger, guilt, your fears.

Become aware of what you're experiencing every moment. Become aware. Acknowledge what you are experiencing. If you don't like what you see, acknowledge it and ask the higher powers to transform it to free you. But, if you say "It doesn't exist within me because I'm too pure, because I've had all these wonderful spiritual experiences..." you will continue to bring your disasters into your lives. Acknowledge yourselves. Love those parts of you and let them go. Know that they've been there to protect you; your jealousies, your fears, your criticisms, all of them have been there to protect you, but you don't need them anymore. But, if you say they don't exist, and they do, that is a lie.

You needn't tell anyone else. Just be honest with ourselves. The more honest you are with yourselves, the more your own light will shine through. Continue to reach for the highest and those parts of ou will fall away and become transformed.

Know that we love you all. It is not easy or comfortable for us to manifest on the physical plane. We love you. That is why we come.

HEALING TRANSMISSION 5: OCTOBER 9, 1986

I ask that you all see clearly. Perceive truth. Learn to distinguish reality from the illusions you create within yourselves, about yourselves, about others. Only in perceiving truth can you walk freely through this lifetime.

Now, bring your enemies into the healing light and love them. Love them until they are no longer your enemies. Bring those who hurt you into the light and realize they too are hurt, they too have hearts, they too are walking the path of earthly existence and have their own suffering, their burdens. Ask to understand and let them go. Bless them because only then will you be freed. Only then. Let them go. Cut the cords of your emotional bondage. The more you think about your hurts the more you ingrain them into your being. The more you put blame outside yourself onto others, the more you create negative attachments, negative strings. They are, truly, if you could see them, strings that are attached to your being and attached to the other person's being, entrapping both of you. Free yourselves.

Trust the universe will bring to you what you need. Know that if you lose something from your life no matter how much you love it, something else, in its time, of a greater nature will come to take its place. The universe has no empty spaces. Trust, even if you walk alone for a while, trust. You will never know what may have transpired with whoever these people are aeons ago in past lives or what you may have done. Accept the situation and make the attempt to resolve, let go, forgive, make it right and free yourselves.

We thank you for enabling us to express once again on the physical plane. Know that you're being watched. Know that you are being guided and trust God always. Know there's purpose for everything you experience. Know that we are here to help you through this journey. Know that this is one of the most important journeys of your lifetimes. The greatest opportunities will be presented to you in this lifetime. Go forth with faith before you. Go forth knowing that God and the universe support you. Go forth knowing that your own higher being, the God within you, goes before you, always, and is preparing the way, is clearing the path. Know this and walk in trust.

HEALING TRANSMISSION 6:
OCTOBER 16, 1986

Know that within you there is a profound place of silence, profound stillness you can go to whenever you need to. Know it exists. All you need do is let go of the mind, breathe, and sit silently. Know that eventually when you become more and more familiar with this silence, you will become the silence. It will begin to emerge through your being, and in the blink of an eye, you can be there. This is your place of peace, your resting place, a place where nothing else exists and where everything exists - you and God.

You wish peace among chaos. You will all be shown how this can manifest in your life. The chaotic will rumble around you and you will be at peace within and fully present to meet the calling of each situation. I ask that in the chaos and in the turbulent times you be fully aware of the higher purpose, and this will bring your peace. I ask that your vision expand to encompass the totality of whatever the situation is, and in those situations, call upon your Father and see them transform.

The greater the lesson, the greater the turbulence, the greater the gift as the outcome. The greater the lesson, the longer it takes to unfold into the gift. So be aware and be patient. Wait and know that when you call upon God, he is there, without question, without doubt.

Observe and know and rest in those times. Be aware and know that your personal wills and your personalities might get in the way. Stay open. Move and decide from the higher impulse. After time, you'll learn to distinguish between the patterned animal self, the programmed subconscious and the higher consciousness. Know that your lives are being guided. Your greatest spirit guide lies within yourself, your own being, and that is the essence of God. Seek that which is within you. Stop seeking outside because when you seek outside, in one way or another, you will always be forced back to yourself.

We send a wave of love to enter your hearts. We wish for you, in this lifetime, to know love in its fullest and purest expression before the lifespans have completed. A great gift. Judge not how that love will manifest. Wish not for it to manifest in any particular way. Love, in its purest is the most wonderful expression. Allow it. Don't program. Don't judge. It doesn't matter whether it is felt for a person, for a painting, for an animal, for an insect, for the sun, for the wind - it will be integrated into your beings.

Think and we will think with you. Think your questions. Ask, and you will know, but you must ask. Ask that the work you do in this lifetime fulfill you. And if it isn't ask to be shown what will and wait and allow the experience and the answer to come in its time. Ask for whatever it is you wish to know and you will receive the answer.

Realize your power. Realize that you draw to yourself whatever you ask for. Listen to the words you speak about yourselves and change them. If there is any detrimental, negative, self-defeating, self-destructive language, your self hears and creates what you say about it. Realize this. Say that you love yourself. Say that you're wonderful. Say that you're loved. Say that you're fulfilled and you will be. Remember this. This is where your power lies. Examine your life now and realize everything you've said has come into being. We leave you with this.

HEALING TRANSMISSION 7:
NOVEMBER 13, 1986

This is a particularly challenging period of time we're living in. The quality of the mass energies, beginning now, will be bringing to your attention, in very graphic ways, the conflicts that live within you. The opposite polarities that live within you. Your need for freedom, your need for relationship. Your desires for health and well being, the self destructive aspects that nag at you like demons, your compulsions.

Realize you're part of the universe and the universe is made of polarity. Light/dark, day/night, life/death, positive/negative, wet/dry, hot/cold and on and on and on. All these systems are also part of your being as you are part of the universe, and personalized in your own unique ways.

In order to manifest your lofty aspirations to help the world, you must first begin to balance the polarities within and make choices, decisions, and then fight the battle of the inner force that pulls you to the personal framework in which you're held back. In which your health, your happiness, whatever it is keeps you back and keeps you from experiencing the fullness of life.

As a suggestion, just for this week to experiment with, make the grand attempt to overcome the self-destructive within you. You know what you're doing each time you do it. You'll be knowing in much more intense ways because the inner forces, both the light and the dark, are emerging and meeting on a different plane.

Within us now is a battle the entire world is going through. What they are going through, we are going through on a personalized level. Each time you overcome another facet of your self destructiveness which you all harbor, each time you do that, you strengthen yourselves and bring more light into the world. You move one step forward in the mastery of yourselves. A frustrating ordeal but the rewards profound. Take control of your life. Take control of your inner being.

You are all intelligent enough to know when you're doing something destructive. It's time to break the patterns that have kept you in shackles. No, it is not going to happen automatically. Much will happen through being exposed to the higher energies, to the healing circle, to whatever teachings your life experience brings you, but you have to do the work. You have to train the inner being onto the path of light and let it know that you will no longer tolerate the self destructive impulses.

Another aspect in freeing ourselves in this world. Another aspect of loving yourselves by choosing what is benevolent. This is one of the challenges every human soul encounters on the physical plane; the choice of continuing with the old ways and letting the self destructive, the animal aspect win. If it does, ill health, unhappiness, constant struggle ensue.

When you are in control and focused for the benevolence of yourself and for the love of yourself you've won the battle of life. You're free. Sooner or later you must all do this. Better that it's sooner, we may not have a later. Better that it's sooner so that these energies can be put back into the cosmos - the energies of transformation, the energies of light over darkness, so all can benefit.

There is the aspect of responsibility for not just yourselves, but for the planet. You can work for the planet through your individual beings. You all count. Any one of you here may be that 'hundredth monkey,' the catalyst for the Great Awakening of humanity. And what better reward than freedom. Do you know what that is? Do any of you know what that is? And yet, that is what you are all seeking.

These are times of constant change, more than you've ever experienced. You can no longer rely on what you have known as security. You will be sustained. You must learn to flow with the universe. Planetary energies are aligning in such a way that the times will be very challenging and yet, the greatest opportunity ever for enlightenment, acceleration.

See yourself stepping into a beautiful river of light. Let the light carry you around the obstacles that come and go. Know you are in the light, safe and protected. You need to have faith and trust. Your higher selves are becoming more and more aligned with your consciousness and your energies are becoming aligned with the universal light.

HEALING TRANSMISSION 8: NOVEMBER 20, 1986

D o you know there is a place within your being that is so peaceful, so wonderful, so powerful, that no matter what is happening in your life, your birthright is to go to this place within and seek your own council and peace. No one can give you what this can give you. Familiarize yourselves with moving inward, with completely letting go of your external world, going within and closing the door. Know that God is there. The place of refuge within you. No thought is necessary. No externals are necessary. You have this available every moment of your life. You don't need candles. You don't need amulets. You don't need incense. You don't need anything but to sit quietly and ask to go to that place, close the door, and be with God.

The more you familiarize yourselves, the more automatic it becomes and the more you can live in this world with all its chaos, all its joy, all the challenges that confront everyone and still be able to retreat and go within where you are untouched and untouchable; where you can bathe in light and come back into the world refreshed, with the same situations taking place - and onward goes life.

When you allow contact with the essence of God within you, which is silence, your outlook changes. You know that regardless of the chaos, regardless of the inner conflicts, regardless of it all, everything is as it should be at this point in time and there is purpose. Gradually, your mind opens more and more and you begin to understand the purpose from the inside out.

I ask that you begin to see the humor in all things and learn to laugh from the heart. That laughter and joy become part of your everyday existence regardless of anything else that's going on. Sometimes we feel that if a terrible thing happens, we're not allowed to laugh - even if there's something funny. It's sacrilegious to laugh. Laugh as much as you can. It is the greatest healing you can give yourself.

HEALING TRANSMISSION 9: DECEMBER 4, 1986

I ask that your guilts, your fears, the remorses within you begin to be seen, lifted and replaced with joy, creativity, enthusiasm and love. I ask that the freedom and joy you experienced as children return to your memory and be relived in your adult lives. I ask that you begin to miss those feelings and be shown how to recreate them again - that you drop the guilts and sorrows and the destructive harnesses that bind you to the past.

There's nothing you can do about it now. Live for now. Live to enjoy your life, what you have left of it. Live to create joy for yourself and that joy will permeate everything and everyone that comes into contact with you, and so, you help the planet. Let this be your responsibility. Let this be foremost in your mind. Know that you deserve it. It is your birthright. No, it is not selfish. It is healthy selfishness and necessary. The world needs it.

Some of you are terrified when you're experiencing joy and try to kill it. You're more comfortable in chaos. You're more comfortable making excuses, holding on to guilt.

I ask that you all be given a vision and experience of what will bring joy and how you can experience it in your life now. It needn't be a sought after, some-time-in-the-future pursuit. Allow yourself to accept it. I ask that you experience the essence of unconditional love so that you know what it is and allow it to open your lives.

HEALING TRANSMISSION 10: DECEMBER 11, 1986

R ealize life is fragile. Look at your lives, examine your lives, and for a few moments place yourself in a position where you are unable to be mobile. From this position, think of what you could have done; the risks you could have taken to enhance your life, to move forward, to create changes. The states of inertia you allow yourselves to fall into.

From this vantage point, think and allow the thoughts to flow through your mind - the ones that have been nagging at you, the things you have wanted to do, places you've wanted to see, people your've wanted to put your finger on the telephone dial and call, creative pursuits you place by the wayside thinking 'someday, someday.'

Let your 'somedays' begin now. Listen to the inner voice, the inner push when it says, here's something that is going to give us joy. Follow its guidance and open your life. There are enough difficult times. Take advantage. Do what is going to enhance, open and give your life more joy and bring more of you into manifestation.

Think about being in that state of immobility and what you've let slip by. Begin to live, appreciate that you can. Be thankful for all the physical resources available to you. It is a blessing, a gift. Thank God that you can speak and make peace and resolve with persons you may be putting this off with.

So many of you feel guilty when you reach out for something that is going to give you pleasure. Something that will be your own thing. There's always another responsibility that pulls you, that calls you. Know that the responsibilities are never going to end. They will continue throughout your life in whatever form they take. You need to deliberately make the effort to reach out, choose and take the risks to develop yourselves. You will enhance your lives and you will still have all the time you need for the other things. Love yourselves in every way you can. Find the true meaning of this and you will find the answer to life. Love yourselves.

HEALING TRANSMISSION 11: DECEMBER 18, 1986

Take in several deep breaths, long and slow, allowing your breath to move you into the silence of yourself. Letting go of all concerns of the day. Place your questioning mind aside for this period of time. Allow yourself a peaceful respite. Be with yourself, moving to the deep center of your being; the place of stillness, the place of peace, the place of power. The place of healing and harmony, the place where you meet God within you. And in that meeting, you expand and become one with the universe and the universal soul. In that place, your words and your thoughts have power and potency. Go to that place with only purity in your heart, in your mind and in the totality of your being.

The period of time we are moving into now is one in which more than ever before, our personal fears will be brought to our attention. Our limitations and the limitations we place on ourselves, on our existence, on our entire being, will be brought to our attention. Thank God for that! The disruption it may temporarily cause will have its reward tenfold in helping to free you so you can experience greater and greater dimensions of awareness and experiences in this lifetime.

Become very aware of your limitations. The times when you feel limited, small, frustrated and imagine a new lifestyle of freedom, of forward movement, of whatever it is that you desire. As long as it doesn't involve the soul or the will of another soul, you're then free to create what you wish.

Ask for answers to your life. Ask for what you want. Aeons ago, a promise was made; if you ask, you will receive. That is a law and that is a truth and it is so simple. Remember to ask and allow the universe, the Infinite Intelligence, to bring the answers to you. Your answers may come in life experience because nothing can be learned by anyone else's words by anyone else's books, through any else's experience but your own. So be prepared to live what you ask and then it will be ingrained in your being. Knowledge is lived.

Always ask for the highest good, that the highest potential may be realized. I ask that the healing touch of God permeate everyone here. I ask that your burdens be lifted. I ask that you have a new awareness.

Realize you can have joy. You can have peace, even amongst the chaos in your life. The two can be present simultaneously. Know this to be true. See yourselves bathed in light. Breath it into yourselves. Know that the light, the essence of God, will do its work silently within you. Know that regardless of what your religion is, there is a consciousness descending, permeating. The Christ Consciousness. The embodiment of God on Earth, manifesting through human form. Know this consciousness is ever descending more profoundly than ever before and its affecting all life on Earth.

You will have your realizations. This consciousness will permeate you. It will bombard you with its truth. Listen. Keep an open mind. Keep open to it. Keep receptive to it. Its essence is love. Its essence is freedom. Its essence and its intention is to make you one with it; manifesting the higher truths, the impulse of God. Perfection on this Earth Plane.

The only way you can free yourselves is to align yourselves with this consciousness, with this presence. It will make itself known to you more and more. The inner animal self will want to fight, realize this. Realize that the deeper subconscious, the programmed computer, wishes to stay programmed. It is safe that way. The unknown is a threat; but to be safe is to be trapped. And so, allow the insights. Know that the tuning fork of the spirit within you will let you know when you are slipping.

HEALING TRANSMISSION 12:
JANUARY 8, 1987

I ask that you have the courage to release your burdens to the Higher Power of God and allow it to do its work. When all that can be done is done, release yourselves. Let go. Free yourselves. I ask that you experience the love and healing presence of God, fully in this lifetime. I ask that you find joy, peace and enthusiasm in your lives.

As you sit here, allow an image of a joyous lifestyle to emerge from within you. Let your imagination give to you what you want in an image; how you want your life to feel, to be experienced. See yourselves free, laughing, loving. See yourselves reaching out and merging with other human beings. Merging in love. Realize you are all part of one family; not recoiling, not isolating yourselves.

You all want, and you are all afraid to reach out and go forth. You only have this lifetime. It doesn't matter about past lives or future lives. Right now is what is important. Move into the ocean of life and swim with it. Don't stand on the shore and wonder and hope. Take the risks. Realize the beauty within you is something that can be shared with others. Realize that you have beauty within you. Reach out. Put your fears aside. Know that you are part of the human family and you are all suffering in one way or another. This is the Human Condition. But, in that suffering and with the burdens and responsibilities, you can experience joy simultaneously. You can!

Honor your life and the planet. It is a responsibility. Set the pattern for others. If nothing else, find that beautiful balance of allowing joy in your life along with everything else.

I ask whether now, in this room, or in your dream state or when you are washing the dishes or working, that an image of joy enter your consciousness and that you hold and create it for yourselves. I ask the presence in this room to stay with you, nurture you and heal you. Anticipate it. Know it is happening and allow it in its myriad of forms.

HEALING TRANSMISSION 13:
JANUARY 28, 1987

I ask that you trust the present circumstances in your lives and not put fear before you. That positive movement and action be perceived, be moved upon and done. Stop trying to force circumstances that are beyond your control. Trust that God within you goes forth from you and prepares the way. That is its job. That is what it has to do.

I ask that you keep your part of the responsibility by keeping your minds and hearts clear, loving yourselves, keeping focused on the positive with faith. Trusting, not fearing disaster. Fear is the Great Destroyer. I ask that your fears be transformed into faith. I ask that you learn to love yourselves and trust the God within you. Trust that every moment, the opportunity to evolve and blossom into all you can be is present.

Trust that if you take the risks necessary in your lifespans, your lives will unfold before you and you will find and reach your potential. Trust that if you do not take the risks and continue to step back in fear, you will fall and be trapped in inertia and fear. Take the steps necessary. Take the challenges that come and love them. Accept change without fear. Experience your life as an exciting adventure you have no way of knowing what is coming next and love that. Love the adventure. Move and go forth with the spirit of adventure and love every minute of it; the pleasant and the unpleasant.

Know that as you progress, your perception will begin to elevate and you will be able to see the value in all your experiences. Know that the fear of death will leave you. Know that even though this lifetime seems to be an eternity, in the Eternal Now, it is a flicker of your eye.

I ask that the spirit of adventure enter into your consciousness and you follow it. Accept the times when, through your personalities, you have made plans, have ordained events to happen at certain times, and when they don't happen as you ordained, trust that the universe and the hand of God is moving in your lives.

HEALING TRANSMISSION 14: FEBRUARY 5, 1987

This is a time of intense magnification of the energies of your lower self (the programmed self) and the higher self (the God self). Both are seeking expression in your lives. The lower self is magnifying, becoming more evident, more easily accessible. It needs and wants to be understood by your conscious self that stands on the middle line between the two; in the center of the Divine Battleground between the higher and lower. Pay attention. Both will be speaking to you very clearly. Pay attention.

Part of your purpose in this lifetime is to recognize and accept these indwelling forces; the two indwelling minds. To master the subconscious and to consciously take control and guide it towards the right and the light. Guide it towards the higher consciousness. Know this Divine battle continues throughout your lifetime. A magnificent challenge and adventure. Know at each step of the way and each moment, you hold control of your choices. The more aware you become, the more options will be available to you, the deeper the understanding, the greater the transformation of the lower to the higher.

Let an image emerge now of your lower self, the child within you, the programmed one, the animal self, the self that is the survival mechanism. The subconscious keeps you alive and protects you. It is your source of physical survival. It has created your body. Know that the subconscious has done it because it loves you; not because it is malevolent or evil. Because it loves you and needs to protect you. It needs to be told that all is well. Its fear needs to be comforted.

Now see an image of it and hold it. Comfort it and tell it that you love it. Stroke it. Love it as you would your own child and tell it that you will be open to hearing and knowing what it is trying to convey through you, through the physical medium, sensations, through the moods, through the events drawn into your life. Put it at peace and assure it that you will recognize it, and make all attempts to. It lives in darkness until it is recognized, acknowledged and loved.

See an image of your High Self, the God within and above you. See it encompassing your life. Know that it lives in the higher consciousness of God; totally benevolent. Know that it goes before you, preparing the way to your freedom. It responds when you acknowledge it and call it into your life.

See it merging with the lower self, holding it in its embrace and transforming the lower self into its light. See it engulf your entire being. See it as a being placing three fingers on your forehead imbuing you with its presence and opening your awareness to its impulse.

HEALING TRANSMISSION 15: APRIL 16, 1987

I ask that you realize and integrate in a conscious way, the knowingness that you create your life and you created all that you have up to this point in time.

In order to create the highest for yourselves, your thoughts must change. Your thoughts about yourself must change. Your thoughts about your role and other people must change. It is necessary to become acutely aware of your thoughts; from the deepest to the most superficial. Become the observer and the watcher, and in your daily waking state, ask the higher mind, your higher self, to bring you to the point of realization where you are continuously aware of what is being created in your life. It is only when you are aware on this level that you can truly be of assistance to another being.

Negativity, pessimism, judgmental attitudes, criticism; these are the poisons that poison you. These are the poisons that create situations of dissonance in your lives. These are the poisons that bring poisonous people and situations into your lives so that you may, once again, see and realize that you have brought this on to yourself.

See everything external as a mirror of yourself. People coming into your life are replicas of something within you that needs to be seen. Do not view them as separate entities who are there to annoy or to disrupt your life. Recognize, even if you don't understand it at first, that they are facets of yourself that you have drawn to yourself to learn from.

Morning, noon and evening prior to going to sleep - practice the ritual of washing your hands three times: Let cool water run over the hands, shake them out and see darkness leave. Ask to be cleansed in your totality. The subconscious will respond. Run the water again, shake the hands. Run the water again, shake the hands and then touch and seal the brow chakra with your hand over the third eye.

All externals are simply mirrors magnetically placed before you for your awareness and transformation. Begin to create the lifestyle, prosperity and the love you wish and anything else you wish for your life. Walk the path of light with intelligence and direction. Know what it is you want to manifest, otherwise you blow like a leaf in the wind.

Yes, we trust the Infinite Mind and we trust destiny, but we don't know what we're harboring within that will be drawn to us. We must create a positive lifestyle so that we understand and realize our role as creators. It is important that we unfold in this way and that the mind is focused on creating a positive, love filled, prosperity filled existence. By manifesting these in your life you can then teach others.

Realize that psychic ability of itself is worthless; absolutely worthless without the working knowledge and knowingness that you are creators and the realizations of how you create your life. This is how you change the world; one by one, having these realizations and putting them into action.

HEALING TRANSMISSION 16: APRIL 30, 1987

Most of you can relate to giving, serving and wanting to do for others. One of the most important things you can learn to do for yourselves, is to receive. Not greedily or selfishly, but with love for yourself. Especially those of you who's lives have been very much outside yourselves; families, giving to others, reaching out, doing more and more in the outside world whether from the heart or for approval, gaining someone's love or keeping someone's love.

You enter the mind set that needs to give in order to be loved. It's true that when you give from the heart you receive much more for yourselves. But many of you have difficulty, shame, guilt with "I don't deserve" attitudes and have difficulty when someone reaches out to give to you.

When you feel that withdrawal, when you feel "I don't deserve this," when you feel "I feel uncomfortable taking," you're denying another person the opportunity to give and you're denying yourself the opportunity to receive. If you allow yourselves to adapt an attitude of open receptivity, opening to God, opening to the universe, opening to prosperity, abundance, healing, allowing yourselves to receive, your lives will become rich.

Many of the blocks you are experiencing will begin to

fall away. You say to yourselves, "I'm so good." "I give and give and give." "I do this and I do that." And yet, the block is there when it comes to receiving. You ask, "Why isn't my life containing love, finances, whatever it is—because you have a block about receiving.

Receiving is not selfish. Allow yourselves. You're not taking anything from anyone. You're allowing energies to interact and flow through you. When you allow this all your innate abilities and more and more spiritual insights, balancing and healing will come through to yourself. So keep this in mind.

HEALING TRANSMISSION 17: MAY 7, 1987

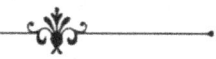

When you are exposed to and in the presence of higher energies, higher teachings, your thinking begins to change The changes that take place are usually imperceptible for the most part. What you're consciously learning and consciously aware of you already know consciously. But there is a certain amount of absorption that is required with each individual. When that level of absorption is reached, chaos takes place, confusion may take place, possibly an onslaught of emotional content that you may or may not know its origin, try to analyze and not be able to. The system may go into moderate, heavy or intermittent states of turbulence. This is the higher knowledge beginning to manifest itself fully within your being.

When an old order is being ushered out, often a crumbling takes place before a new and strong foundation is built. When light enters and shines its presence upon darkness, darkness is illuminated and you can see what is in the darkness. This is disturbing, and should be. It is part of the process. If it is happening, accept it because those facets of you, which are in states of imbalance, need to be released or need to become aware of by you consciously so that you, once again, are called to be master of your life, creator of your life. The one who stands above and is able to see the content within and direct the activity from a conscious place.

This is a process that happens so be aware and be thankful, not alarmed. It will pass to a higher inspired state, and on and on and on and on.

Now, whoever we place in the circle tonight for healing - it is important you know that each individual has chosen and manifested the condition and the state they're in. It is important that you know they will be touched in some way and not attach yourselves to the end result, to looking over your shoulder to see if healing has taken place. Each individual has their own time schedule, as does God, and we can't determine what that is. We can only allow an opening and be vehicles and vessels.

HEALING TRANSMISSION 18: JULY 1987

I ask that the spirit and essence of healing be present. When this is called upon it is a reality that exists. Your words have power. Your thoughts have power. When you're in a meditative state and you speak with sincere intent, there's a response from the universal energies. So, we ask that healing be present. I ask that each one of you be touched, be opened in some way. I ask that you open to greater creative ideas to move your life along the path. I ask that you open to the higher consciousness within yourselves and recognize its impulse within you.

Know that there is an intelligence, a force within you that loves you. It loves you in a way that no earthly person can love you. It is beyond what you think of as love. It is complete unconditional love. It is within you and outside you. It is your deeper consciousness, your higher consciousness, your true spirit guide in this lifetime. It holds the knowledge of what will benefit you, what will free you and bring you into a peaceful existence beyond the chaos you presently exist in.

Listen to the higher impulse that may go against your patterned responses. Do something different. Approach your challenging situations in a different way. Listen, because you're being guided every moment of your existence, whether you're awake or asleep. That's guaranteed. It is your birthright and you will know if you open your inner ears to listen.

It doesn't come to you in advance of any situation. It is there the moment you need it. It is always there if you listen. It will express right action, right attitude. And so the wise person, who truly wants to be free, trusts and goes along with it as foreign as it might feel. Only when you break the robot-like patterning will you establish a new order of benevolence, creativity and freedom in our life. You have your guidance with you at all times.

HEALING TRANSMISSION 19:
OCTOBER 1, 1987

This coming year is going to be a year of very powerful transformation. There will be times when you are going to be thrown into states of confusion, borderline intense decisions needing to be made almost out of nowhere. Situations will arise with 'split decisions,' ones where you are not going to know what to do. Do not become distressed with this. The energies that are manifesting will be creating situations like this. In these times it is important that you pull into yourselves, step back and wait, giving yourselves permission for a brief waiting period.

I'm resisting saying this because my questioning mind is saying: How can this happen to everyone in the room. There are too many people for the same thing - and yet, for some reason it's coming through for everyone here.

There's an opening taking place within your consciousness that is going to allow powerful communication with your higher selves. The higher mind is seeping through and the lower mind will be in rebellion while this process is taking place. It is a strong transformative healing process. You are all going to be lifted and aligned with a higher level of consciousness, reaching the point where you will be self-taught by this higher guidance.

And so, pay close attention to when the lower unconscious rebels because there will be rebellion. There will be a battle. Many times the battle will be against what you consciously know is the right path to take, what you consciously know is good for you, what you consciously know is going to open your experiences and create change.

The lower self comes wants to maintain its security and safety with the known established patterns. The lower unconscious does not want change. The higher consciousness is change; always positive, ever forward moving change. It always leads you to your highest potentials, always leading you to your highest good.

Be aware of the forces within you. Acknowledge them. Accept them. Love them. Find the central place within you, the place of silence you can retreat to, the place of peace. Give yourselves permission to retreat to your center so you can come back into the world with the strength and stability that you can only find in this peaceful place. Regardless of the chaos, regardless of the conditions, regardless of the situations, you can find this within you. It's your birthright. You need to be able to consciously say, "I let go." Walk away from the situation. Find a place and retreat. You can do it. It's possible.

HEALING TRANSMISSION 20: OCTOBER 29, 1987

Follow your own rhythm. Be aware of and follow your own rhythm. Follow the inner promptings within. Begin to put the 'should' aside and allow yourselves slowly, step by step, to attune yourselves back to your natural rhythm.

Don't fight sleep when sleep calls you in the middle of the day. If it's possible for you to sleep, allow it. If you have planned an activity and don't feel like doing it and something else comes in, don't do it. Begin to tell yourselves: "I want to live naturally now." Tell yourselves you want your natural rhythm to manifest. Realize you've been going through life as a patterned, programmed robot much of the time and going against all that's natural within you.

It is important to begin to come back to yourselves, attune to yourselves, and whenever possible give yourselves pleasure. Allow yourselves to nurture yourselves. No one else can do it for you. The more you honor your own inner rhythm, promptings, and intuition, the more your life will flow. If you fear you won't accomplish what you are setting out to accomplish within a day or a week or whatever the case is, you'll be surprised that you will accomplish all of it and even more because everything has it time.

Look at nature. Learn from nature. Nature is effortless as it becomes all that it is.

Healing Transmission 21:
November 19, 1987

Know that the new era and age of awakening is here. A very highly refined level of energy is descending and bearing down onto the Earth. Its essence is healing. You will be called upon to stop and take stock of yourselves. A very personal search is going to be taking place within everyone. Moment by moment your guidance will be available. It is a time when your personal guidance will be there but it may not be there in the way you would like it to be - like a booming voice coming out of the heavens and telling you what to do. It will be there in subtle ways. Your body will speak to you of its needs. Your body will speak to you of what it needs for balance. Pay attention to what your body is telling you when you become aware of imbalances, of blockages of things that are not in balance and attend to them.

Your minds will be filled with conflicting thoughts. The thought and the impulse of the mind of God is here. The Teacher is here. The change has taken place. The event that everyone for aeons has been waiting for is descending on us now. It's here. This is the time. The time is now.

It is important to begin to think in terms of following your natural rhythms and impulses. This may mean doing things in ways you wouldn't ordinarily. Breaking sleep patterns. Changing eating patterns. Your body will tell you what it needs. One of the keys will take place through the physical body. Listen to it.

You will notice a stronger inner voice that may not appear to be any different than your own thought at first and so, you might ignore it. You see, you are God and God is your thought and the thought is there. Pay attention to the thoughts that come from nowhere, unannounced. Listen to them.Ponder them. If you're given direction, take risks and move in those directions. Especially when the body needs rest, give it rest so you can integrate and keep balanced in this changing time.

You will notice intuitive thought heightening. You will notice the reaping of your thoughts, many times almost instantaneously, the positive and the negative. Focus your minds on the light. Focus your minds on creative pursuits. Focus yourselves on creating the beneficial in your lives; alleviating and cutting through your fears. The realization of fear as an illusion is one of the greatest things of importance to be realized at this time.

Creativity will heighten. Ask your questions when you are in a confused state. Take the time to sit quietly and focus your mind on asking the question that will evoke guidance. Focusing your intent is very important so that your minds don't run away like wild stallions The guidance you seek will be there. This is one of the major components of what is happening and what is going to be happening. Guidance will be there from within yourselves and more accessible.

HEALING TRANSMISSION 22: JANUARY 28, 1988

Your lives will be going through radical shifts and changes. Lifestyles will be going through rapid changes. You will be taken out of current situations, predicaments; what has been the known, what has been your point of security. You will be led into greater areas where you can express yourselves more fully and experience the creative evolutionary processes within yourself and environments.

You are all responding to the silent call that you've come into this Earth plane and have been waiting for. It is very important to listen to the new thought patterns that are being instilled within you. Each one of you are being changed at a rapid rate. New thought patterns are being established within your consciousness. Expect periods of confusion where you will attempt to grasp what has been secure for you, what has been known, what has been an existing pattern that you felt safe in. Then, at the point of grasping for it, the veils will lift from your eyes. You will see the non-prodctivity of the old that you've immersed yourself in and will be given instantaneous awareness of the more creative path to take which you will be compelled to take.

Fear nothing. You are being guided. All of you here, at one point in your past existences, experienced the freedom of life in other dimensional existences where thought was instantaneously manifested. All of you have experienced lifetimes on this planet, Earth, in which you have also mastered your intent for creativity, for harmlessness and for good. Where your thoughts held their highest power to manifest. You have forgotten and have come into this life deliberately blocking the memory of those existences so that in this most intense period of Earthly existence, you will rediscover what you've forgotten and had mastered within yourselves.

Pay close attention to the new thoughts and patterns that emerge because they are emerging in all of you. Write to the extent that you can, when these thoughts are recognized. You will see the pattern we speak of by bringing it forth through the written word so that it doesn't remain in the confusion of the mind.

There is nothing to fear.

If you could see the reality of what we speak of, you would be perceiving your lives as the most exciting adventure. You would know, in the deepest part of your being, that all of you here are part of a group that upon physical death, will be returned into the creative light. You cannot fall from grace. You walk in grace, blinded to it presently.

Allow yourselves to take the leaps and the risks. Allow yourselves to experience the changes that will transpire in each of your lives. Look forward to it. Fear nothing. There's nothing to fear.

HEALING TRANSMISSION 23: AUGUST 9, 1989

This is going to be a time of heightened emotional response. What is happening now is that so many of you are not feeling your emotions or reactions. It takes something major to make you feel. You suppress them or are always somewhere else you really don't know what is going on.

The universal energies are coming in through the brain into the solar plexus and stimulating quicker, more dramatic, more felt emotions. Whatever has been dormant, ignored, but still present, is going to be coming up and becoming visible. Expect your reactions will be changing.

The quality of the energy, the cycle, and the changes, are saying that this is a time when we need to be completely honest, acknowledge ourselves fully. Not make excuses, not justify, not say "Oh, that is not like me." It is saying that we need to become fully aware of who we are so we can allow the multitude of changes that are constantly taking place in us to be felt. It is going to be a very erratic time but a very exciting time. The opportunities for breaking free will be there.

When you experience these things you may begin to take on guilt. This is not appropriate. What is appropriate is to acknowledge what is present as it is. You are in for many surprises about yourselves. You are going to see changes in people that will be very surprising and you are going to experience these changes within yourself as well.

The true nature of everything is being brought out into the open where it can be seen. It's not that the person has changed. It's not that you have changed. This is a universal energy that will break up whatever has been crystallized, suppressed, ignored and denied. Honesty is going to be required and tolerance is going to be required.